STANDING IN
Grace

*Living in the New Testament
Message of Grace*

By David Guzik

*The grass withers, the flower fades,
but the word of our God stands forever.*

Isaiah 40:8

Table of Contents

Dedicated to Inga-Lill
An amazing gift of grace to me
and to many others

Chapter One

Whatever Happened to Grace?

In Him we have redemption through His blood, the forgiveness of sins, according to the riches of His grace. (Eph. 1:7)

Browsing through a magazine rack in the public library, I noticed one headline that caught my eye: "Christianity and Mental Health."[1] It was the feature article in that month's edition of *The Humanist* magazine. Curiosity got the best of me, and I sat down to read the essay.

I didn't expect a sympathetic treatment of the issue, coming from a magazine with that title, and the author, Wendell W. Watters, met my expectation. After twenty-five years of practicing psychiatry he'd come to the conclusion that Christianity destroys the mental health of society and individuals. He explained his thinking in the first paragraph:

> I want you to entertain the hypothesis that Christian doctrine, the existential soother par excellence, is incompatible with the principles of sound mental health and contributes more to the genesis of human suffering than to its alleviation.[2]

The rest of the article attempted to prove his point. It wasn't hard for any thinking Christian to see that Watters was on the wrong track, and his case didn't stand up. But as I read what this seemingly angry, bitter man wrote about Christians, I felt an unexpected reaction: *agreement*. In more than a few places, I found myself agreeing with this determined critic of Christianity. While elaborately weaving half-truths with valid insights, the author also managed some striking observations. I noticed that he didn't describe how the Christian life was *meant* to be experienced, but how many people *really did* experience it. For example, Watters noted:

> Christians are taught that only God can assign value to individuals by saving them from their sins. By flagellating themselves emotionally and proclaiming their intrinsic worthlessness and emptiness, Christians try to manipulate God into feeling sorry for them and saving them.[3]

Apart from the psychiatric doublespeak, Watters meant that many Christians beat themselves up emotionally and spiritually, hoping God will feel sorry for them.

In examining prayer, Watters wrote:

> [Prayer] demonstrates how Christianity tends to reduce its adherents to a state of the abjectly whining, cajoling, coercive infant—whether the goal of a particular entreaty is good weather, relief of pain, the welfare of souls dearly departed or simply storing up brownie points with the divinity.[4]

As a pastor, I knew what it was like to help many Christians who felt the same way. They had changed what God said about our real need for Him into something that kept them in constant guilt and depression. For these believers, God's love was more to be *earned* than *received*. Apparently, Watters had met these kinds of Christians, and he took their experience as true Christianity.

> A true Christian, steeped in the doctrine of Original Sin and in Christ's sacrifice on the cross, is expected to win favor with God through all manner of verbal breast-beating, fault-finding with self, and confession of sin.

A true Christian must always be in a state of torment, since he or she can never really be certain that God has forgiven him or her for deeply felt negative feelings—in spite of the Catholic confessional and the fundamentalist trick of self-deception known as being saved or born again.

[The Christian is] doomed forever to fragmentation and abject groveling at the feet of the divine Big Daddy.[5]

With that perspective of "true" Christianity, it isn't any wonder that this writer for *The Humanist* concludes:

It is a tribute to the resilience of the human animal that anyone subjected to this kind of indoctrination week after week, year after year, can grow up with any degree of self-acceptance, let alone self-esteem.

This breast-beating, self-flagellating behavior represents a form of good old-fashioned blackmail and, unfortunately, is a form that creeps into all too many interpersonal relationships.[6]

It was easy to see that what Watters protested against wasn't true biblical Christianity, but it was also evident that many people struggle with the type of Christian life he described. I had to admit that sometimes I dealt with the same false conceptions about God and the Christian life—I struggled with a vision of God and His work for me that brought bondage instead of liberty. Though the pseudo-Christianity that Watters attacked isn't biblical, it's the *experience* of far too many sincere Christians.

What was missing? What was the difference between the destructive faith criticized in *The Humanist* and the abundant life offered by Jesus? I've come to believe that what Watters described—and what many believers experience—is a *graceless* Christian life. This kind of Christianity is far more common than I realized, and it doesn't just affect Christians who feel worthless before God. Graceless Christianity also impacts those who feel pretty good about their relationship with the Lord.

Eligible for Blessing

Most people think of *grace* as an old-fashioned word, representing an unfamiliar concept. Grace seems to lack the pizzazz of the latest spiritual fad or wind of doctrine. It reminds us more of senior citizens humming "Amazing Grace" than a new generation trying to find their way. However, an understanding of grace, or the lack of it, *directly* affects our everyday relationship with God. What the Bible says about His grace answers two questions that are rarely spoken yet constantly asked: (1) What does God *want* from me? and (2) How does He *feel* about me?

On any given Sunday at virtually any church, you'll see Christians who suffer because they answer these crucial questions wrong. Looking beyond casual talk about the weather and the recent ball game, past the auto-pilot smiles and "just-fine" replies, you'll see believers who desperately need a better understanding of grace.

Some come to church with unbridled excitement and expectation. They simply know they'll get what they're looking for from God; after all, they're the kind of people God loves to bless. They've probably come off of a good week, with no major sin and an adequate fulfillment of the Ten Commandments. They read their Bible and prayed some that week. Perhaps they've even had the tremendous experience of sharing the gospel with someone. Whatever the reason, "eligible for blessing" seems to be written all over their faces. Because they've been the right kind of people, they assume that God is fair and will do right by them. Good seed has been planted, and now these eligible ones expect to enjoy all that's rightfully theirs. As they arrive at church on Sunday morning, their joy is genuine, and they can't wait to steer the conversation onto what they recently did or experienced that was so pleasing to God.

But on this same Sunday morning, at the same church, there will most certainly be those who feel they're *not eligible* for blessing. These believers live the kind of harmful Christian experience described by Wendell Watters in *The Humanist*. They are, at least at the moment, haunted by the realization that this isn't how they're supposed to feel. So, they do their best to look like others think they should look. As prayers are offered and singing begins, the feeling that they've disqualified themselves from blessing on that particular morning is hard to shake.

Mary, for example, is a dedicated Christian woman. She comes to church week after week and greets everyone with the smile that good Christians are expected to give and receive. But many of her Sundays are spoiled by the belief that God isn't quite pleased with her. For example, on this particular Sunday, she knows she lost her temper with her children on Thursday, and she feels terrible about it. She's convinced that her lack of self-control, and the resulting guilt, mean that God has nothing good to give her today. Mary feels this way this often, even when she can't think of any specific thing she's done wrong. Considering herself disqualified from God's blessing, she knows this is a Sunday to be endured more than enjoyed.

When Mary feels like this, she looks at others with a mixture of envy, admiration, and despair. Everyone else seems so spiritual and so ready for a touch from God. But because of a bad morning or a bad week, the disqualified like Mary have an unpleasant sense that they must pay a price for their wayward living. The dry harvest of bad seed that's sown days before must be endured, and a better crop is hoped for in the coming week.

Think of someone sitting next to Mary—we'll call him Tom. Tom feels completely different than Mary, though you wouldn't necessarily know it from his outward appearance. Though Mary feels ineligible for blessing, Tom feels quite eligible because he had a *great* week with the Lord. He had a blessed devotional time with the Lord almost every day, and he even spoke to a co-worker about Jesus. When Tom gets ready for service, his attitude is, *I think God will bless me today because I had such a great week.*

Both the eligible and ineligible sit together in the same pew, exchanging cordial greetings. They might even be husband and wife. Whoever they are, they experience worship and hear the sermon quite differently, but neither one may experience them the way God intends. The person like Tom believes God's blessing is inevitable because he's been such a good Christian. The person like Mary knows she's messed up before God and that blessing is impossible. Both Tom and Mary are probably living a *graceless* Christian life.

It's easy to see how someone like Mary needs to understand more about God's love and grace. But how can it be bad to feel good about ourselves? That kind of self-confidence certainly feels better than the weight of self-imposed guilt and depression. However, those good feelings can be just as harmful to our spiritual health as the painful feelings of ineligibility. A confident sense of personal worthiness underlies an attitude we might call "assertive" or "optimistic," but God may see it simply as pride. We may feel confident with such a positive perspective, yet we may also be in a dangerous place, heading toward self-reliance and making it easy to reject God's day-to-day participation in our life.

Both the "up" and "down" attitudes are common, and it's not unusual for Christians to bounce between extremes from week to week. Either mindset may cause serious problems in our spiritual development, presenting difficulties that aren't unique to Sunday mornings. These difficulties may extend to seemingly everything that touches our fellowship with God. Yet both attitudes are corrected by an understanding of what the New Testament says about grace. Mary and Tom's problems share the same root—they're based on a graceless Christianity. Each perspective is poisonous for a healthy, mature Christian, and they must be corrected by an understanding and application of grace.

What Happened to Grace?

Grace is God's answer to the sense of chronic frustration and its flip side of self-reliance. Yet grace in the Christian life isn't the topic of many sermons today. It's not that the doctrines of grace are despised by believers (though some, in ignorance, do reject them); they're more often simply ignored. Many mistakenly see grace as a basic principle, quickly graduated from in their experience. Others lose what God says about grace in the confusion of the latest fads among Christians.

Many preachers and teachers do teach grace and consider it relevant today. Still others fail to understand or communicate its principles. For these, grace may be a popular buzzword, but it's not genuinely applied.

Perhaps the greater problem has to do with how theologians treat the concept of grace. Many scholars use the word *grace* as a handy catchphrase, whose definition describes almost everything relating to the Christian life and almost nothing relating to practical living. A theologian's lofty explanation of grace may be meaningful for other intellectuals, but it's often useless for the man or woman in the pew. Fortunately, there are solid scholars who remain sensitive to the importance of grace in understanding the Bible; but again, their audience is often only fellow scholars and seminary students. Therefore, the power of grace is made irrelevant by defining it as either a too broad or too narrow way. And the strength of grace is useless if it's locked away in large books with too many big words.

Those who talk about grace may use glowing terms when describing the salvation of souls, but they frequently ignore the transforming power that grace can have in helping us understand more about God and ourselves. For these, grace is only necessary at the beginning of the Christian life. Others who teach or write about grace are apparently afraid of it. Their discussions are usually a prelude for telling us to guard against any teaching that encourages people to sin.

Because some preachers fear that focusing on grace will encourage others to sin freely, grace is presented only halfheartedly. What's given with the right hand is taken away with the left. This kind of teaching inoculates against grace. It offers a small, watered-down dose of the truth—just enough to make us think we know all about it. A halfhearted presentation of grace contributes to graceless Christianity.

But we don't have to live that way. When the church misunderstands grace, it either finds itself cursed with Christians who are weak, timid, and insecure or with those who are proud and self-reliant. Yet we *can* embrace the truth of grace from those complex and distant theology books and place it within the hearts and minds of believers who are hungry for God. When that happens, a personal revolution occurs. Christianity flourishes when we take the grace of God seriously; we begin to see revival in our own lives, as well as in the church.

What Grace Can Do

You need to know more about God's grace if you feel:

- discouraged or disqualified from blessing
- proud and self-confident
- tired of an up-and-down Christian life
- inadequate before God and others
- enslaved to the opinions of others
- fearful and insecure
- powerless in battling against sin

A greater understanding of God's grace can provide the key to victory in each of these areas of struggle. This means taking a fresh approach to the subject of grace by letting the Bible speak with its inherent power. In this way, we can seize upon the same sense of grace that the writers of the New Testament came to recognize as their own.

Toward the end of the 20th century, the great Scottish preacher Alexander Maclaren declared:

> Now that word "grace" played a much larger part in the thoughts of our fathers than it does in ours; and I am not sure that many things are more needed by the ordinary Christian of this generation than that they should rediscover the amplitude and the majesty of that old-fashioned and unfashionable word.[7]

Living about the same time as Maclaren, English preacher Charles Spurgeon challenged his hearers in a sermon on 1 Corinthians 15:

What do *you* know about the grace of God? "Well,
I attend a place of worship regularly." But what do
you know about *the grace of God?* "I have always
been an upright, honest, truthful, respectable man."
I am glad to hear it; but what do you know about
the grace of God?[8]

A generation later, James Moffatt wrote in his remarkable book,
Grace in The New Testament:

Indeed, few better services could be rendered to
Christianity in these days than to retain and if
possible to re-state the significance of grace as the
New Testament writers sought to grasp it.[9]

These men knew the Christians of their generation had to
reclaim recognition of the great doctrines of grace and apply these
truths in their full strength. This need was evident in their day;
it's even more apparent in our own. There's far too much graceless
Christianity being lived today.

Fulfilling that need requires both an exploration of what the New
Testament writers say about the grace of God, and an application of
what the Holy Spirit has said to our lives today. However, to do so
we must begin at the beginning: what *is* grace?

Chapter Two

Amazing Grace

And if by grace, then it is no longer of works; otherwise grace is no longer grace. But if it is of works, it is no longer grace; otherwise work is no longer work. (Rom. 11:6)

Graceless Christianity is a problem. Understanding and receiving God's grace is the solution, but many Christians have a limited understanding of what grace is.

According to Steve Turner in his book *Amazing Grace: The Story of America's Most Beloved Song,* in December 1999 the newspaper *USA Today* suggested several items for a turn-of-the-millennium time capsule. The collected items would communicate the essence of the twentieth century to the future. The items included Barbie dolls, a can opener, a Chevy Camero – and the song sheet for "Amazing Grace."[10]

Though the song "Amazing Grace" sung by Judy Collins became a top-10 hit on the American music charts in 1971[11], there is a sense in which the 9-11 terrorist attack made the song seem even dearer to Americans. Turner notes:

> The song was used at church services, memorial gatherings, tribute concerts, and funerals. It was played on Manhattan's Fourteenth Street by a

Salvation Army ensemble as volunteers loaded trucks of supplies for helpers at Ground Zero. Pipers from NYPD piped it at the commencement of the Prayer for America service held at Yankee Stadium. Red Cross workers sang it at the site at Shanksville, Pennsylvania, where United Airlines flight 93 had plunged into a field after its hijackers were apparently overwhelmed by courageous passengers.[12]

For many Christians, the most meaningful and eloquent expression of the work of God's grace is stated in this famous song. Perhaps you can quote the verses by memory, but for a greater blessing, read them carefully:

Amazing grace! How sweet the sound
That saved a wretch like me!
I once was lost but now am found
Was blind but now I see.

'Twas grace that taught my heart to fear
And grace my fears relieved;
How precious did that grace appear
The hour I first believed.

Through many dangers, toils and snares
I have already come;
'Tis grace hath brought me safe thus far,
And grace will lead me home.

"Amazing Grace" is indeed a great song about God's grace. But the glory of grace must be more than sung; it must also be experienced in our lives. Interestingly, the man who wrote this favorite hymn was, in fact, one who was profoundly touched by the grace of God. His name was John Newton.

After trying to desert the Royal Navy as a young man,[13] Newton found himself on a ship headed back to England by way of Canada. Off the coast of Newfoundland, his ship ran into a terrible storm. The situation became desperate—from 3 a.m. until noon, Newton was forced to operate the pumps that kept water from sinking the ship. All provisions were thrown overboard or spoiled, and there was little hope for survival. Newton felt exhausted and deathly afraid, and he didn't know how to swim. In this time of great fear, darkness, and dread, he remembered his godly mother. Then, somewhere off the coast of Newfoundland, Newton came to the end of himself and was converted. Meanwhile, the ship passed through the storm into calmer waters.

Even after his conversion, Newton remained captain of a slave ship, but his eyes were eventually opened to the inhumanity of what he did. So he left the slave trade, became a pastor, and eventually worked to make slavery illegal in the British Empire.

At the age of eighty-two, the former slave-shipper summed up his life by saying, "My memory is nearly gone, but I remember two things—that I am a great sinner and that Christ is a great Saviour."[14] Newton's life had genuinely changed by his understanding of God's amazing grace.

Unfortunately, even though "Amazing Grace" is considered our country's most popular hymn, few Christians know God's grace in the wonderful way that the author of this hymn did.

The Meaning of Grace

If you feel limited in your understanding of grace, don't be discouraged; it probably isn't your fault. This generation hasn't had enough good teaching on grace, so if you have a hard time understanding it, you're in good company.

One noted theologian of ancient Christianity, Augustine of Hippo, felt at a loss for words when describing grace. Even as a deep thinker and scholar, it is thought that when someone asked him what grace was, he answered: "What is grace? I know until you ask me; when you ask me I do not know!"[15]

When theology experts talk about grace, they often use complicated terms; however, understanding what the Bible says about grace doesn't have to be mysterious.

Toward the end of his first term as president, Ronald Reagan held an elegant state dinner for Francois Mitterrand, the Prime Minister of France. As a butler led the President and Prime Minister to their table, Mrs. Mitterrand suddenly stopped. She turned to President Reagan and calmly said something to him in French. He didn't understand, and both Reagan and the butler motioned to her to go forward, but again very calmly, she repeated her statement to the President.

An interpreter finally explained the problem—the President was standing on her gown![16] A failure to understand had caused a brief moment of embarrassment. But our failure to understand what grace is about can have eternal consequences.

Many theologians misunderstand grace when they fail to emphasize that the grace of God is *personal*. It's more than a description of God's action or His power to help us; it describes how God *feels* about us. Grace, as the New Testament teaches, isn't a cold, technical word; it's filled with the warmth of God's love and affection. Seeing grace in abstract, overly technical terms leads to exactly the kind of graceless Christianity we should avoid.

What the Word *Grace* Means: Its Non-Christian Usage

When the Apostolic writers, inspired by the Holy Spirit, began to write the Gospels and letters of the New Testament, they used the ancient Greek word *charis* to describe the Christian concept of grace. If we want to understand what the New Testament means by the term *grace*, we must begin with an understanding of what charis meant to its ancient users.

A fine wine has many distinct flavors and nuances of taste, and it's the job of a wine taster to assess and distinguish between these subtle differences. In the same way, important words also have various flavors and nuances, and good "word-tasters" carefully study these distinctions to gain a full understanding of these words.

One of the strong "flavors" of the word *charis* is "that which awakens pleasure or secures joy."[17] In ancient times, if you went to a chariot race and the entertainment of the contest was pleasing to watch, you might say the chariot races had charis because they brought you joy. Moffatt put it well when he wrote, "What rejoiced men was called *charis*."[18] In modern times, we use a similar word that expresses this thought. If a person has a magnetic personality or a unique charm, we say that person has *charis*ma, which is taken from the same Greek word.

Charis also conveyed the idea of *beauty*, a beauty that gives pleasure and awakens joy within us. Even today, we say that a dancer or athlete who moves beautifully is graceful, or full of grace. We use the word *grace* for people or things with beauty and style. The person marked by grace is considered lovely and elegant, and we think of them as having no blemish or deformity.

The word *charis* was also used in association with supernatural power or aid.[19] In the literature of ancient Greece, charis was sometimes seen as a mystical power that supernaturally influenced the personality of man with its goodness and beauty. Sometimes this was thought to be like a magic spell, unseen and supernatural yet full of power. It was common for the ancients to think of the gods (or God) bestowing this supernatural grace upon man.

Finally, the word *charis* conveyed the idea of an unmerited, undeserved favor or attitude of kindness. It was regarded as the active expression of unselfish aid and help.[20] The famous Greek philosopher Aristotle defined the word in this way:

> Helpfulness towards someone in need, not in return
> for anything, nor that the helper may get anything,
> but for the sake of the person who is helped.[21]

Charis could be used to describe an unexpected blessing or a treat, such as an unforeseen gift or benefit. The purpose for giving a charis gift was found in the giver, not in the one receiving it.

We should recognize an important difference between the common usage of the word *grace* and the way the New Testament uses this word. The ancient Greeks knew of grace and they valued it, but they thought of grace as a favor only exchanged between friends. The idea that one might show this great favor, beauty, supernatural help, and undeserved kindness to an enemy was completely foreign to them. Popular Greek scholar Kenneth Wuest says:

> In its use among the pagan Greeks it referred to a favor done by one Greek to another out of the pure generosity of his heart, and with no hope of reward.... In the case of the Greek the favor was done to a friend, never an enemy. In the case of God, it was an enemy, the sinner, bitter in his hatred of God, for whom the favor was done.[22]

When Paul and the other New Testament writers used the word *charis*, they retained its associations of joy, favor, beauty, supernatural help, and undeserved favor. We must keep all these "flavors" in mind as we study such an important New Testament word.

The great Bible teacher G. Campbell Morgan offers this description of grace in his commentary on the book of 2 Corinthians:

> It first meant everything in the realm of beauty, as against ugliness, of strength as against weakness, of health as against sickness, of love as against hate. The aesthetic realm, the realm of beauty and glory and health and strength, all that is high, as opposed to all that is low—grace, *charis*. Then in later writings it took on a new meaning, and it was the desire to impart these to other people. I am referring still to Greek literature. Then these New Testament writers took hold of it, and lifted it into a higher realm, and it became a word standing for the activity that fulfills the desire to impart the things of health and beauty and glory, instead of shame, to other people.[23]

Wuest wrote powerfully about the relation between the classical understanding of charis and the New Testament use of that word:

> The Greek word for "grace" is a wonderful word. Archbishop Trench says of it, *It is hardly too much to say that the Greek mind has in no word uttered itself and all that was at its heart more distinctly than in this.* When the word is brought over into the

New Testament one can repeat Trench's statement, substituting the word "God" for "Greek." *It is hardly too much to say that God has in no word uttered Himself and all that is in His heart more distinctly than in this.*[24]

Charis was a popular word in the New Testament, especially with the apostle Paul. All the letters he wrote begin and end with "grace to you" in some form. Paul was so taken with the concept of grace that he even invented words from the root of charis. One such word is *charismata*, which Paul called "grace gifts" and we usually call "spiritual gifts." Without a doubt, charis and the ideas behind it were essential to the gospel that the apostles preached. Moffatt says:

> The religion which underlies the New Testament writings is a religion of grace, or it is nothing.... No grace, no gospel; that is what it comes down to, when you study the classical documents of the primitive church.[25]

Charles Ryrie also recognized the centrality of grace to the Christian faith when he said, "Without grace, Christianity is nothing."[26] The motto of the early church, and especially Paul's ministry, was "All is of grace, and grace is for all."[27]

Grace: God's Unmerited Favor

Perhaps the best-known description of this important New Testament word is that grace is God's unmerited favor. This definition has become somewhat of a cliché, but it's an accurate and helpful starting point in coming to a useful understanding of grace.

We say grace is *God's* because the Bible teaches that grace is an essential aspect of His character. Simply observing how He deals with individuals and nations in the Bible shows that He is a God of grace. For example, His choice of Abraham and the nation that would come from him wasn't based on their goodness or worth, but on His powerful grace. Nothing in them merited the special status of God's chosen people. Granting this favor showed that God was gracious in His dealings with Abraham and his descendants. They often tested God and rebelled against Him, but He kept showing His incredible grace and amazing patience with Israel through the wilderness journey. Even when God corrected Israel, He did it as an expression of His love for the nation.

God specifically speaks of Himself as a God of grace. When Moses went up on Mount Sinai to receive the Law, he asked for the privilege of seeing God. God showed Himself to Moses with power and glory, declaring a title that revealed His character. Moses learned about the kind of God who had delivered them from Egypt:

> *And the Lord passed before him and proclaimed, "The* Lord, *the* Lord *God, merciful and gracious, long-suffering, and abounding in goodness and truth."* (Exo. 34:6)

The God of Moses and Mount Sinai was a gracious God of mercy and kindness. Moses knew for certain that the God who would lead them across the desert was full of grace and mercy.

The way God deals with people expresses His gracious nature. Even in judgment, He shows grace. When the city of Jericho faced God's judgment by the armies of Israel, God showed His grace by sending spies to offer believing Rahab a way of escape from the coming judgment. She was a Gentile prostitute, but God showed favor to the unworthy, even in the midst of well-deserved judgment.

The Bible shows God to be a giving God who gives life, love, mercy, forgiveness, healing, power, guidance, and deliverance to people who don't deserve these things. This aspect of His nature that gives to the undeserving can be called *grace*.

We also see the God of grace through the life of Jesus. Jesus perfectly revealed God's nature and attitude, and that revelation was filled with grace. In the introduction to his gospel, John says, *"Grace and truth came through Jesus Christ"* (John 1:17). Jesus was the embodiment of the Father's personality; He completely exemplified grace as He walked among men. He openly invited undeserving sinners to know God and have relationship with Him through the person and work of Jesus. God's grace in Jesus drew men away from their sin and self and toward God Himself.

Grace is a characteristic of God in His triune nature. The Bible describes the Father as the God of all grace:

> *But may the God of all grace, who called us to His eternal glory by Christ Jesus, after you have suffered a while, perfect, establish, strengthen and settle you.* (1 Peter 5:10)

We're told in John 1:14 that Jesus is the revelation of grace:

> *And the Word became flesh and dwelt among us, and we beheld His glory, the glory as of the only begotten of the Father, full of grace and truth.*

And in a passage of warning, the writer to the Hebrews says that the Holy Spirit is the Spirit of grace:

> *Will he be thought worthy who has trampled the Son of God underfoot, counted the blood of the covenant by which he was sanctified a common thing, and insulted the Spirit of grace?* (Heb.10:29)

Grace is an essential aspect of God's nature, and all true grace comes from Him. In the New Testament, grace is certainly *God's* unmerited favor.

Getting What We Don't Deserve

We say that grace is unmerited because its giving is not earned by the one who receives it. The reason for giving grace can only be found in the giver, who is God. Paul says plainly in his letter to the Romans:

> *Now to him who works, the wages are not counted as grace, but as debt.... And if by grace, then it is no longer works; otherwise grace is no longer grace. But if it is of works, it is no longer grace; otherwise work is no longer work.* (Rom. 4:4, 11:6)

Paul states it simply: Grace cannot be earned in the same way that wages are earned. If grace is earned in *any* way, then it isn't grace anymore. Grace has absolutely nothing to do with the worthiness of the one who receives it.

Let me illustrate with an imaginary situation.

John and Joan are both good Christians. One day John tells Joan, "Joan, because you are such a good person, I'm going to give you a dollar."

Is that grace? No, because John is giving to Joan because of some merit or goodness that's in her. Sure, John is being *generous* and *kind*, but he isn't displaying the kind of grace that the New Testament describes.

Now it's Joan's turn. She says, "John, I know you hate biting your nails and you've been trying to stop. You're doing so well, I'll reward you with a dollar."

Is this grace? Of course not. Again, Joan's giving is prompted by something John has done (or stopped doing). In the same way, God's grace isn't given because of what we do or don't do for His sake.

Giving is only of grace when Joan gives because she *wants* to give. The giving can have nothing to do with what John has done or what he promises to do in the future. As mentioned, John and Joan are both good people. In fact, John might be so good that he *deserves* a dollar. But if Joan is giving from grace, it doesn't matter if John is good or not; she gives because she likes to give.

God, in His grace, is that kind of giver. Grace doesn't care if you're deserving or not. It doesn't say that you don't deserve it (as we will later see, the *law* says this); rather, grace says that your deserving has nothing to do with God's giving. Grace is given to the deserving and undeserving alike, because God refuses to look for a reason to give to the receiver. Grace is given without any thought of merit on the part of the one who receives. Its cause and motivation are only in the giver.

If grace isn't treating a person as they deserve, it's also not treating a person *better* than they deserve. Joan could say to John, "John, you're good enough to deserve fifty cents, but because I'm a giving person, I'll give you a dollar."

Many people believe this is how God's grace operates. They believe we deserve just a little bit from God (perhaps we've earned it because of our faith or repentance), and that grace means God gives a lot when we deserve a little. That's not grace at all, because the principle of deserving is still present. John deserves something; Joan merely gives him more. Grace deals with us completely apart from the principle of deserving. As Charles Ryrie says, "Grace by its very nature can involve no merit."[28]

In Matthew 20, Jesus told a story that illustrates how God's giving isn't based on man's deserving. This parable—like all parables—isn't meant to teach a whole system of theology. It emphasizes a specific truth: God's right to give out of grace, not according to man's idea of who deserves a reward.

Jesus spoke about a landowner who needed laborers to work in his vineyard. Very early one morning the landowner hired several workers in the marketplace and agreed to pay them a denarius (the standard day's wage for a working man). Later, about 9 a.m., he went out and hired more workers. At 12 noon and again at 3 p.m. he persuaded still more men to come and work for him. Finally, at 5 p.m. he found more willing workers and he hired them. To all the workers he hired from 9 a.m. on, he simply said, "Whatever is right you will receive." When the working day was over, he started to pay his laborers, beginning with those who were hired latest in the day.

Even though those who were hired last had worked only one hour, the landowner paid them a denarius—a full day's wage. I can imagine how excited the workers were who had started at the beginning of the day. When they saw the men who only worked a few hours getting paid for a full day, they probably thought, *If the landowner pays them for a full day's work, he'll probably pay us for two or three days. After all, we worked two to three times longer than those latecomers.* Yet as the landowner paid all the workers, he gave each one a full day's wage, whether their working day had started at dawn or at noon.

When the men who were hired at the very start of the day

received their wages, they complained. They thought it was unfair that they'd worked all day and received the same pay as those who had worked only an hour. Then the landowner said to these complaining workers:

> *Take what is yours and go your way. I wish to give to this last man as much as to you. Is it not lawful for me to do what I wish with my own things? Or is your eye [heart] evil because I am good?* (Matt. 20:14-15)

This parable isn't a perfect illustration of grace, because the principles of working and deserving are involved. But what it does show about God's grace is enough to make most of us uncomfortable. In the parable, God appears to be unfair. After all, shouldn't the people who worked longer get better pay? Isn't a day's worth of work better than an hour's worth? But what Jesus showed was that God can give to a man or a woman out of the riches of His goodness, *totally apart* from what they deserve. To be truthful, the men who only worked an hour didn't *earn* as much pay as those who worked a whole day, but the landowner chose to give it to them, and he could if he wanted to.

What if you found out tomorrow that someone at your workplace was given a huge bonus, above and beyond their normal pay? Of course, you were paid exactly what you expected, but your co-worker received this unexpected gift. Perhaps you'd been with the company longer, perhaps you'd had more responsibility, and perhaps you'd even worked harder than your happy co-worker; yet the boss gave *him* the bonus instead of you. How would that make you feel? Would you be happy with your co-worker or would you be angry with your boss? Most people would probably respond the same way that the first workers in Jesus' parable did—by resenting the generosity of their boss.

Many of us take this same attitude toward the Christian life, and we actually despise the grace of God when it's given to others. Perhaps we have a secret feeling that such unmerited kindness should only be shown to *us*. Remember that your boss may not have the authority to show such unmerited favor to any employee, but the point of Jesus' parable is that God *does* have that right. The King of Kings can justly deal with men and women on the basis of grace, apart from what they may or may not deserve. There's no question about God's right; there's only a question of our response. Will we respond to God's sovereign grace with resentment or rejoicing?

The unsettling aspect in this parable and its presentation of grace is that we generally *like* the system where everybody gets what they deserve. It's predictable and safe. After all, it's noble to refuse charity and earn your own keep. Under the rule of "You only get what you deserve," there's never any doubt where you stand in the world, and there's no doubt about how you got there.

However, we should never forget that God's kingdom isn't run on a principle that demands everyone must *earn* their way. Although God does recognize and reward devoted service, He's under no obligation to give or bless according to our deserving. This is why the person who trusts in Christ and receives salvation on their deathbed is allowed to go to the same heaven as the one who serves Christ faithfully for eighty years. From man's perspective, this isn't fair or right, but in the eyes of God, it displays the glory of His grace.

God Likes Us

Finally, we say that grace is God's unmerited *favor*, because that tells us how God *sees* and *feels* about the one to whom He gives His grace. He sees that person in a favorable light. In Paul's day, the word *grace* (charis) was used to describe the emperor's favor by which he would bestow gifts and kindness upon the cities and people of the Roman Empire.[29] To receive the emperor's charis meant that you were held in special regard by the emperor of Rome. To receive God's grace means that you are held in special regard by the God of the universe. This is His attitude toward those who receive His grace. He *likes* them!

We can see this more clearly by looking at the word *disgrace*. When we're dis-graced (not graced), we don't enjoy favor and aren't seen in a good light. At that moment, all we know is shame and degradation—no honor, glory, or approval. Fortunately, the believer is not *dis*-graced but is graced by God. The Christian enjoys God's favor and pleasure, and this is prompted by His gracious, giving nature, apart from any work or ability in the one believing.

This is a difficult truth for many to accept. We may come to the point where we freely believe that God loves us, but it's harder to believe that He *likes* us. After all, we love some people yet we don't particularly like them because they irritate us or get on our nerves. Family relationships are often like that. For example, we realize we don't like Uncle Charlie and we prefer to not be in his company, but since he's family, we have a love for him and send him a card and fruitcake every Christmas.

Because we're aware of our imperfect devotion to God, we may easily think that His attitude toward us is the same. We may think He loves us because we're "family" and He has to love us, yet we fear *He doesn't really like us*. God's grace assures us that this isn't true. God our Father doesn't love us merely out of some sense of family obligation. He doesn't find us irritating, nor does He barely tolerate us. Rather, when He looks at those who are in Jesus Christ, He sees beauty, and it awakens joy and pleasure within Him. *You* are beautiful to Him.

Keeping these truths in mind, we see that grace is God's unmerited favor, but it's also much more. Alan Redpath spoke to this point:

> Now what does that word *grace* mean? You have often heard it defined as the unmerited favor of God. Well, that is a definition, but it is only a limited definition of the word.... Now the word has taken on many different meanings down through the years. When this word was used in the early stages of history, it meant a desire to bring to other people goodness, health and strength, beauty, and loveliness. Later it became a little more pregnant in its meaning and began to mean the actual activity which expresses the desire to bring to others goodness instead of

evil, health instead of sickness, beauty instead of ugliness, glory instead of punishment.[30]

When our eyes are opened to the meaning and importance of grace, the Bible takes on new meaning. Grace is no longer simply a vague, impersonal force that's somehow responsible for salvation; it describes the *attitude* and *approval* God extends toward me. We notice that the Bible is suddenly filled with examples of God's gracious acts and descriptions of His attitude of grace toward the believer. We see that the New Testament constantly speaks of the believer's standing in grace and the need to continue in grace. The practical application of these New Testament doctrines of grace can be life-changing, because God's grace is life-changing.

Chapter Three

Saved by Grace

For by grace you have been saved through faith, and
that not of yourselves; it is the gift of God, not of works,
lest anyone should boast. (Eph. 2:8-9)

Predestination or free will? It's a question that consumes the time, intellect, effort, and agony of many theologians, amateur, and professional. The one-word reply of "predestination" or "free will" (generally identified with "Calvinist" or "Arminian") supposedly reveals your viewpoint on a variety of doctrinal issues. In some ways the differences between the two camps are profound and irreconcilable, but in other ways the differences are superficial and semantic.

For example, all Christians would (or should) be able to properly answer the question, "Why are you a Christian?" with the response, "Because God has shown His grace to me." That's an important foundation that all Christians can agree on, whether Calvinist or Arminian. But our agreement seems to stop there, leaving us an argument with two sides and no end!

The whole debate is actually about the role of grace in getting people saved. Theologians like to use the term *grace* to talk about God's part in getting us saved. Calvinists (the predestination people) view salvation as a work of God's grace, *resulting* in the cooperation of man's will. Arminians (the free will folks) see salvation as a work of God's grace, *requiring* the cooperation of man's will. Each side believes that *both* God's initiative and man's response are combined as features of the salvation process; however, they disagree greatly as to how those features work together.

This book is about grace and how we can live in it. We'll leave behind the discussion of man's contribution to the process of salvation and focus on God's part. And as we do, we should avoid a trap that many theologians (professional or amateur) easily fall into. We must remind ourselves that grace isn't some vague, impersonal force unto salvation; it's the unmerited favor of God. Grace is more of an *attitude* than a *power*. Of course, since God is God and He is sovereign and omnipotent, His attitudes are filled with power. Yet we should avoid the trap of thinking of grace as some kind of impersonal force.

Saved from What?

One of the most eloquent statements in the Bible concerning God's grace and salvation is found in Ephesians 2:8-9. First, it tells us we're saved by grace. The concept of being saved is familiar and good, but we often fail to understand or communicate what we're saved from. To say that one needs to be saved implies that they're in danger and will be harmed or destroyed if they aren't rescued. But what do we need to be rescued from? Huge books have been written on this subject, but we can condense a basic answer into a few paragraphs.

The New Testament tells us at least four things we can be rescued from in Christ, and the first is *sin*. When the angel Gabriel told Mary she was chosen of God to miraculously conceive and bear the Messiah, he gave her specific instructions concerning His name:

> And you shall call His name Jesus, for *He will save His people from their sins.* (Matt. 1:21, italics mine)

The first and perhaps the greatest thing grace saves us from is sin. It's our sin that separates us from God, distorting and defacing

His image in us. In one sense, the very root of sin is selfishness. It's been noted that at the very center of sin is "I." That self-seeking, self-willed desire infects every aspect of man's being and world.

Before his career in politics, Abraham Lincoln was a prominent citizen of Springfield, Illinois. One day his neighbors heard the screams of his children in the street. Alarmed, one neighbor rushed out of his house and found Lincoln there with two of his sons, who were both crying uncontrollably. "Whatever is the matter with those boys, Mr. Lincoln?" the neighbor asked.

"Just what's the matter with the whole world," replied Lincoln, with a note of sorrow in his voice. "I've got three walnuts, and each wants two."[31]

Lincoln's remark has the ring of truth. The source of virtually every evil in us, and in the world, is self-willed desire. God's plan is to change our hearts from self-interest and give us access to the power we need to defeat sin. The root of every problem among us is either the direct or indirect result of sin, but by His plan of grace, Jesus came to rescue us from sin and the tyranny of self will.

We're also saved from our enemies. When Zechariah, the father of John the Baptist, prophesied about the coming Messiah, he said:

> And [God] *has raised up a horn of salvation for us…*
> *that we should be saved from our enemies, and from*
> *the hand of all who hate us.* (Luke 1:69, 71).

There's a coming day of total peace and rest for every godly person, when all persecution will cease and every enemy of the gospel will be silenced. Until then, God promises to rescue us from the power and authority of *the* enemy: Satan, the enemy of our souls. Satan's skills have been honed by ages of experience; however, he's a foe who's already disarmed in light of Jesus' work on the cross. In Colossians 2:15, Paul tells us that through Jesus' victory on Calvary, He "*disarmed principalities and powers*" and "*made a public spectacle of them, triumphing over them in it* [the cross]." The principalities and powers described are none other than demonic powers united in opposition against Christians. Jesus has disarmed these forces, making the way of victory available to us through the cross and He offers this in His plan of grace.

The devil isn't our only enemy; the world system also fights to conform us into its image. We live under a constant barrage of ungodly attitudes and values that mark our society. Whether we feel it or not, we're targets of this world's conforming influence. Our submission to fads and fashions, along with admiration of the world's heroes, shows how much we're affected by this influence. Fortunately, the power of God's grace is able to save us from the enemy of the world and its conforming power. Peter, in his sermon on the day of Pentecost, told us this:

> And with many other words he [Peter] testified and exhorted them, saying, "Be saved from this perverse generation." (Acts 2:40)

The world is merciless in its attempt to unite us in an anti-God frame of mind, but through Jesus we can be rescued from this perverse generation.

So far, we've seen that we can be saved from the three classical enemies of our faith: the world (*this perverse generation*), the flesh (*our sins*) and the devil (*our enemies*). But there's something else we must be rescued from, and Paul speaks of it in his letter to the Romans:

> Much more then, having now been justified by His blood, we shall be saved from wrath through Him. (Rom. 5:9)

The wrath that Paul speaks of in this passage is not the wrath of man, but the holy, righteous wrath of God. How did we ever become targets of this anger? Because we submitted to the desires of the flesh, the rebellion of the world, and the deceptions of the devil; we set ourselves squarely against God and His will. We became guilty of treason against God and are fully deserving of His wrath.

People don't understand or believe this today. According to the way many think, God would be unfair to show His wrath toward anyone, much less toward anyone they know. Hell is thought to be a place reserved for a few of the most notorious men of history, but those who live normal lives are thought to have a free pass to heaven. God is no longer considered a righteous and fair judge; He's been replaced by a grandfatherly god whose only distinctive attribute is a bland kindness.

This isn't the God of the Bible. The Bible tells us that every human being is rightfully deserving of the wrath of God, and if it weren't for His offer of salvation through Jesus, everyone would be under that wrath. We should never assume that God's mercy and grace somehow cancel out His righteousness and justice. Rather, God's plan of salvation is so great that it provides a way of *escape* from His wrath, without contradicting His righteousness. Therefore, when we come to the Father through Jesus, according to His plan of grace, we're rescued from the wrath of God that we fully deserve.

But what are we saved *from*? When we place our faith in Jesus, we're rescued from the domineering oppression of the world, the flesh, and the devil, as well as from the righteous wrath of God. Tragically, many are ignorant of their need to be rescued from these dangers. The god of this age has blinded their eyes (2 Cor. 4:3-4), and they cannot see their need or the provision of Jesus.

Grace in the Person and Work of Jesus

Though we may agree with our need to be saved, how does grace make salvation possible? First, every Christian would agree that we're saved by the person and work of Jesus, and His person and work are an example of God's gracious love toward us. The apostle John tells us that "*the Word became flesh and dwelt among us…full of grace and truth…. Grace and truth came by Jesus Christ*" (John 1:14, 17). Or in other words, when Jesus became a man, he lived out God's grace.

The fact that Jesus *came* proves God's undeserved love to us. Did mankind, either as a group or individually, *deserve* that departure from heaven? Was there a popular vote on earth to reform us for the coming of the Messiah? Did God look down from heaven and say, "My, there's a group of people who are so good that they deserve a Savior"? Of course, these thoughts are ridiculous. Jesus came into a hostile, God-hating world that was steeped in sin. He didn't come because we *deserved* a Savior; He came because God loves lost people.

Not only did the coming of Jesus show God's grace, His whole life showed grace. Interestingly, Jesus never used the word *grace* in His teachings (except in the sense of thanksgiving). Later, through the apostle Paul, God revealed specific teaching about grace. And even though Jesus rarely used the word, He often taught about the idea of grace. More importantly, His life and ministry exemplified God's grace in action. His love for sinners and social outcasts clearly showed God's unmerited favor. The tax collectors, prostitutes, and other sinners Jesus befriended didn't receive His love because they were worthy, but because grace was lived out through Him.

If Jesus had only shown God's love to those who deserved it during His earthly ministry, no sick people would have been healed, no demoniacs delivered, and no sinners forgiven. However, His entire life and ministry were marked by God's grace.

And yet grace was most powerfully displayed by Jesus' death. No one can read the gospel accounts of Jesus' arrest, trial, and crucifixion without noticing that He died for the undeserving. No one did anything to earn such a display of love, but God gave it out of the treasures of His grace. At Calvary, God showed forth the riches of His love in the greatest measure. In contrast, the sin and hatred of humanity was also shown at Calvary in its blackest degree. What could be worse than people taking joy in murdering the God of perfect love and righteousness? At the cross, the best of God's love and worst of man's hatred met and did battle, and Jesus' empty tomb proclaimed that God's love and grace emerged victorious.

Jesus' death on the cross not only shows us the grace of God, it also *allows* grace and forgiveness to be given to the believer without any violation of God's righteousness or justice. This is an important and often misunderstood aspect of Jesus' work on Calvary. God couldn't say to a rebellious people, "Oh well, you're off the hook by My grace." That would have been a complete violation of His righteousness and justice. We wouldn't think much of an earthly judge who decided to let lawbreakers off the hook simply because the judge happened to be in a nice mood that day. We would rightly say that such a judge was incompetent and should be removed from the judicial bench. In the same way, God didn't let us off the hook at the cross; He put Jesus "on the hook" for us. The judgment we rightly deserved was poured out on Him as He stood in the place of sinful humanity. The cross didn't sidestep God's justice; it satisfied His righteous law. The penalty was paid by Jesus instead of the believer. So the cross allowed God's grace to operate for man's salvation, without violating either His righteousness or His justice.

The day Jesus died on the cross was a day of judgment. Jesus, who knew no sin, was made sin for us (2 Cor. 5:21), and He took the judgment that sinners deserve. But there's also a coming day of judgment before God's great white throne. All who stand before Him on that day will be judged and condemned if their names are not found in the Book of Life. Today, God offers all of humanity the opportunity to choose their day of judgment. If we decide to trust in Jesus and repent of our sins, then all our sins will be considered as judged in Jesus on the cross at Calvary. If we decide to reject Him and hang on to our sin, we will be judged at the great white throne of God and will bear our penalty ourselves. The great truth to realize is that God's righteousness requires that *all* sin must be judged, and it will be. However, we have the privilege to either choose to bear our own penalty for sin or receive the substitutionary work of Calvary, thus being saved through Jesus Christ.

We've seen how the incarnation, the life and death of Christ our Savior, displays God's grace for humanity. God did all these things for an undeserving people. But the truth of the empty tomb is different because there is a sense in which Jesus was not raised from the dead primarily for our sake; it simply had to happen. Jesus' resurrection was inevitable. He was raised from the dead because He *did* deserve it. That was not a product of God's gracious love for mankind. Even as the Father could righteously judge the sin of man as it was placed upon Jesus, so also He could not righteously allow Jesus to remain in death.

In the sermon Peter preached on the day of Pentecost, he recognized this principle when he perceived that the psalmist David was prophetically speaking the mind of Christ when David said:

> *For You will not leave my soul in Hades, nor will You allow Your Holy One to see corruption* [decay]. (Acts 2:27)

Jesus had done nothing wrong when He bore the sin of the world. In fact, it was the greatest act of love and self-giving of all time. Therefore, it would not be fair or righteous for Jesus to remain bound by chains of death, and the Father could not let His Holy One rot in a grave. Jesus deserved to be raised from the dead in triumph and glory.

So resurrection was inevitable for Jesus. But because of grace, we can share in His victory over death. God would have been entirely justified in reserving the power and benefits of the resurrection only for Jesus. He deserved that victory over death and we do not. But by God's remarkable grace, He allows us to share in Jesus' triumph over death by granting us the promise of resurrection and eternal life. Christ's resurrection glory is a preview of ours; He is the firstfruits of the resurrection.

Grace in Our Salvation

Not only does the person and work of Jesus show us grace, but God allows us the opportunity to experience the work of grace in our individual lives. This work of God in us shows that salvation is of grace. Most of us went through weeks, months, or perhaps even years of preparation before we made a decision for Jesus Christ. Why did God work on us for so long? We should all wonder, *Why would God choose me? Why would He work on my heart, making it sensitive to the gospel? Was it because I deserved it?* When we honestly examine ourselves, we can only answer no.

God didn't search to and fro across the earth to find someone worthy of salvation and then choose you or me. The reasons for His choosing rest entirely in Him. He chose to prepare our hearts for salvation because He wanted to, not because we deserved it. Perhaps there were specific circumstances that led to your decision to follow

Jesus. Why did God arrange those circumstances? Because of His grace. Thankfully, the Bible tells us we are "*justified freely* [we don't have to earn it] *by His grace through the redemption that is in Christ Jesus*" (Rom. 3:24).

The fact that our salvation rests on the foundation of grace is extremely comforting. Unlike faith or works, grace is a sure and steady foundation for our salvation. Our faith may waver, our works may fluctuate, but God's grace stays the same. If salvation were founded upon my faith, I'd wonder if I was saved every time I experienced doubt. If it were based on my good deeds, every sin would call eternal life into question. But salvation is based on the grace of an unchanging God. What a relief that is; what peace and rest it brings!

By Grace, through Faith

The next thing Ephesians 2:8-9 tells us about our salvation is that we're saved through faith, and that faith is not of ourselves. This brings up a point that may seem merely technical, but it's actually vital to our understanding of salvation and grace. Notice Paul doesn't tell us we're saved *by* faith, but that we're saved *by* grace *through* faith. This is an important distinction. The work of our salvation is accomplished by grace, and saving grace is received by faith. God gives what theologians like to call "common grace" to everyone. Matthew 5:45 says that the rain falls "*on the just and the unjust alike*" (NLT). But the riches of saving grace are reserved for those who will receive that grace by faith. Paul echoes this thought in Romans 5:2, where he tells us that our access into grace is by faith. And so, it is only by our faith that we come into this position of grace (undeserved favor resulting in salvation).

When we say we receive grace by faith, we must remember that faith isn't a deserving work by which we earn grace. There's a danger of thinking of faith as a work by which we earn God's favor. Genuine faith will bear the fruit of good works and can't be separated from them; this is what much of James' letter is about. Although good works accompany true faith, faith by itself is not a work. Faith merely sees God's offer and believes it to be true. It looks at the promises of God and says, "I believe they're for me." In simple terms, faith is *refusing to call God a liar*. It's taking God's Word at face value and trusting that both He and His word are reliable. When we don't have faith, we deny that God's Word is true and call Him a liar. What merit is there in *not* calling God a liar? That's only common sense.

There's a story about a man who taught a Sunday School class full of small boys. One day he offered a boy in the class a brand-new wristwatch. The boy thought it was a trick. Fearing his classmates would laugh at him when the trick was revealed, he refused the watch. The teacher then offered the watch to the next boy, but this child followed the example of the first. One by one, each boy refused the watch because the offer seemed too good to be true, and each one believed the teacher wanted to trick them. But when the teacher offered the watch to the last boy, he was bold enough to accept it. And when the teacher actually gave the watch to him, the others were amazed—and angry. The teacher used the situation to show them that no matter how good a gift may seem when it's offered, those who receive it must believe the word of the giver and receive the gift before it can do them any good.

In 1829, a Pennsylvania man named George Wilson was sentenced by the United States Court to be hanged for murder and robbery. President Andrew Jackson pardoned him, but Wilson refused his own pardon, insisting that he wasn't truly pardoned unless he accepted the pardon. That was a point of law never raised before, and President Jackson called on the Supreme Court to decide. Chief Justice John Marshall gave the following decision: "A pardon is a paper, the value of which depends upon its acceptance by the person implicated. If it is refused, it is no pardon. George Wilson must be hanged," and he was.[32] In the same way, God's offer of pardon and salvation in Christ Jesus is offered to many, but only those who trust God and His word will gain the benefits of that pardon.

Our response of faith is important to the working of grace because it completes the connection. If I choose to give you one dollar out of grace, you must receive that dollar by faith before it can do you any good. If you don't have faith in my offer, then the offer does no good. The same principle of receiving grace by faith is at work with salvation. We must believe and receive for the connection to be complete. But first we must empty our hands of what we're holding on to if we're to receive what God wants to give us.

Preachers like to tell the story about the boy who once got his hand stuck in a vase. His parents tried everything to get it out, but the hand remained stuck and the boy started getting scared. Finally, it seemed that his parents would have to break the vase to free the hand. Just before they were to break it, the boy asked, "Would it help if I let go of the penny I'm holding?" In the same way, until we let go of whatever petty thing we're holding on to, we can never be free and receive by faith.

We usually have our hands so full with what is false and with serving ourselves that we can't receive God's offer of salvation. That's what repentance is all about. It's emptying what is false and wrong in ourselves so that through faith, we can receive what God has to give us.

Ephesians 2:8-9 tells us that this faith is *the work of God in us*. We wouldn't even have the faith to believe and receive if God didn't previously accomplish that work in us. Therefore, we understand all the more that faith cannot be a deserving work that earns grace unto salvation—faith merely receives it. In Acts 18:27, Luke describes a group of converts in the early church as *those who had believed through grace*. Their belief—like all true faith—was a work of grace in their lives, accomplished by God.

Not of Works

Finally, in Ephesians 2:8-9, Paul tells us that God arranged this system so none can boast that their own great works brought them salvation. Think of what a horrible place heaven would be if salvation were of works instead of grace. Everyone would brag about how faithful they were, about how many they had led to Jesus, and how much they'd given for His cause. There would be a lot of false humility and arguments about who is the most humble. We should thank God that He decided to work out salvation in a manner that silences all our boasting.

Our problem is that often we *want* a salvation of works so that we can brag, even if only in the inner person. We may do good works in order to prove to others what a good Christian we are or how "saved" we are. It goes against our natural desire to appreciate a system where salvation is given and boasting is silenced. This is why the natural man, apart from the work of God, hates grace and the system of salvation based upon it. Grace takes no regard of what we deserve, only of God's gracious giving. Grace denies any expression of our pride. It tells us that we owe everything to God, and that He owes nothing to us. James Moffatt said it like this:

> "Grace" suggests that one is under an obligation to
> God, whereas the unwritten creed of many is that
> God is under obligation to them, or at any rate that
> He is to be used rather than adored.[33]

This is why the proud refuse to come to God by His appointed system of grace. Proud people assume they already have God's favor and that there's no need to receive the salvation Jesus brings.

- Pride demands to be seen in its merits; grace refuses to aknowledge them.

- Pride considers itself better than others for superficial reasons; God's grace sees all people as equal.

- Pride gives the self preeminence; grace gives God preeminence.

Is it any wonder that "*God resists the proud, but gives grace to the humble*"? (James 4:6). The humble are willing to receive God's grace unto salvation because they recognize their need before God and are willing to come to Him on a basis that ignores their merits. The humble realize that to come to Jesus, they must come on the grounds of His grace and not on the foundation of their works. Therefore, it also follows that Christians who are proud are also blind. Believers who are proud don't understand that they're accepted by God in the grace and merit of Jesus alone, without looking to whatever they think they deserve by their goodness.

How Do These Truths Apply?

First, we must recognize that the great secret of the Christian life is to believe and consent to be loved *while unworthy*. Many people put off receiving salvation because they don't feel worthy of it. Others never receive God's love because they're convinced that they're undeserving of such a gift. Grace tells us this: the fact that we're not worthy doesn't matter. Grace isn't grace unless it's given without thought of merit in the one to whom it's given. As Moffatt said when reflecting on the apostle Paul's understanding of grace: "Only those who are prepared to acknowledge that they are unworthy, can put their faith in the Giver of grace."[34] In other words—you don't need to *seek* God's grace; you need to *accept* it, for it is offered freely to those who will receive it by faith. Many people go their entire lives without knowing God's grace because they won't receive it unless they *feel* that they've earned it. Grace that must be earned is not grace at all. Don't be fooled by the lie that tells you to wait until you feel deserving. When you do feel deserving, then you're in danger of pride.

If you've put your trust in Jesus unto salvation already, then rejoice in your salvation of grace. God has designed the system of grace so that it glorifies Himself and not man. Therefore, your appropriate response to receiving salvation is to praise the God of such grace. And as you praise Him, vow to serve the King of your salvation in gratitude for all He's given you.

If you *have* received this grace, which is the basis of your salvation from sin, take care that you do more for grace than you ever did for sin. Do sinners love their sin more than we love the God of our salvation? Does the world serve sin more eagerly than we serve our God of grace? We should commit ourselves to a stronger love and more complete service, not to earn God's favor, but to show our gratitude for such favor received.

Chapter Four

Standing in Grace

Therefore, having been justified by faith, we have peace with God through our Lord Jesus Christ, through whom also we have access by faith into this grace in which we stand, and rejoice in hope of the glory of God. (Rom. 5:1-2)

One evening the famous scientist Albert Einstein attended a dinner party. Einstein's neighbor, who was a young girl, asked the white-haired professor, "What is your profession?"

Einstein replied, "I devote myself to the study of physics."

The girl looked at him in astonishment, "You mean to say you study physics at your age? I finished mine a year ago!"[35]

Perhaps you have the same attitude toward the grace of God. Many Christians get the message that they finish with grace soon after conversion and then should move on to deeper truths. If that's how you think, don't feel bad. It may be the result of what you've been taught. But this thinking robs many Christians of the abundant life Jesus promised.

Yes, we're saved by grace. Yet the work of grace doesn't end when we're born again. People who think the work of grace is for the past and not the present are likely to be victimized by graceless lives. They don't understand that we're not only *saved* by grace, but we also *stand* in grace.

First Things Always

God never intended that His work of grace should merely give us a start in our Christian life. In the Bible we read about the importance of standing in grace, continuing in grace, and never departing from grace as the principle that guides our lives. Continuing in grace means we're to live with the realization that God's favor and affection are ours because we're in Jesus Christ. Grace says that God cherishes each one of us as His beautiful, prized possession and that He will always love and care for us. As we've already seen, God feels this way about us because of who He is, not because of who we are or even what we promise to become.

Paul repeatedly warned Christians that they must not depart from grace, and he *"persuaded them to continue in the grace of God"* (Acts 13:43). Of course, Paul preached that salvation was of grace (Eph. 2:8), but he thought grace was also important *after* the altar call. Grace is the *principle* by which Jesus' followers are meant to live their lives. This principle that saved us is the same principle that should mark our Christian walk from beginning to end.

For this reason, some of the strongest warnings in the New Testament are to those in danger of falling from grace (as in Gal. 5:1-4). Peter knew the importance of grace in the present tense when he wrote: *"This is the true grace of God in which you stand"* (1 Peter 5:12). Clearly, to the earliest Christians, grace was to be the constant standing of a disciple of Jesus and not just the way to begin the Christian life.

A Tragic Departure

For some reason Christians find it all too easy to leave grace in the name of growth. When the church seems troubled by a crisis, an emphasis on grace may seem like a luxury. Sadly, many early Christians soon departed from the simple teaching of life in grace. After Paul and the other apostles left this world, it wasn't long until some Christians began disregarding the warnings of the Spirit that were meant to ensure that they continued in grace. They failed to recognize that we're told to "grow in the grace and knowledge of our

Lord and Savior Jesus Christ" (2 Peter 3:18), not to grow away *from* grace or grow *beyond* grace.

In the decades after the apostles died, writings began to appear that showed a departure from the New Testament teachings on grace—writings that tended to carry on the legalistic principles of Judaism. This was a direction toward the Phariseeism that distressed Jesus greatly. Some prominent Christian teachers tried to preach a strong morality so that the church would have a spotless reputation. But in their emphasis on personal performance, they neglected Jesus' indwelling grace as the foundation for right living.

Before long, sects began teaching that there could be no cleansing or return to God's favor if a Christian sinned after being baptized. Other groups believed that only one "major" sin was allowed and after that, there could never be forgiveness or restoration.

Some taught that Jesus had paid the first installment on our moral debt to God, and by this He freed us from the moral bankruptcy court. But they also said that once we are set free, *we* must keep up the payments on our debt! In trying to keep Christians pure, many people started thinking the path to Christian maturity meant *earning* our way to God.

This kind of attitude continues among many Christians today. When the church speaks to the problem of sin in the Christian life, it often departs from grace, only to find that rules and regulations have no real power to restrain the flesh. The church then often slips into legalism, which promotes a moral zeal but takes us away from understanding that salvation is the free gift of God, given by grace. This makes salvation something we must earn or deserve, at least in part. In his book, *The Doctrine of Grace in the Apostolic Fathers,* Thomas Torrance summarized this attitude:

> The new life in Christ is not conceived of as a gift, but something to be striven after during a period of probation in which men are subject to strict conformity to Law.... For these Christians, salvation has become a doubtful case of enduring to the end.[36]

This is the attitude of graceless Christianity, which isn't the

Christianity of the New Testament. Clearly, the Bible tells us that grace is a *standing* and *permanent principle* in the Christian life, not merely an introduction. James Moffatt emphasized this truth:

> An essential element of the apostle's teaching upon grace is that this attitude of receptivity towards the gift of God is not a preliminary phase but a standing condition.[37]

The child of God is not only initially saved by grace, but is also "kept saved" by grace. Paul rightly insisted, "I do not set aside the grace of God" (Gal. 2:21). The Christian *stands* in grace. An unbiblical and graceless view is that the start of the Christian life is in grace but the maintenance of salvation is our job. This unscriptural teaching tends to go further in its denial of grace. Someone who denies that the Christian *stands* in grace will eventually deny that the Christian is truly *saved* by grace. This happened for many believers in the generations after the apostles.

Staying in Grace

How can we stay in God's grace? How do we avoid the strong tendency to grow away from grace instead of growing in grace? First, we should understand that God gave a path of access into a standing of grace. In Romans 5:2, Paul says our *access* into this standing of grace is by faith. This word *access*, describes the introduction or ushering of someone into the presence of royalty.[38] By faith, we have access into the favor of the King.

I sometimes wonder what it would be like to rub elbows with the rich and famous or with the movers and shakers of our world. I remember when my friends used to go to rock concerts and their most prized possession was a backstage pass because it gave them access to the stars. They were privileged to go where others couldn't go. When the sign said, "Authorized Personnel Only," they knew that they were authorized. But really, having access to the politician or celebrity of today would be nothing compared to meeting with the King of Heaven. That is truly privileged access, and it's the right of every Christian by faith.

Paul used emphatic wording in Romans 5:2, and literally he wrote, "We have access as a permanent possession."[39] Our path of access to God is permanent and will never be denied. It isn't temporary. Our right to entry won't be revoked. A standing condition of favor and acceptance is ours as those who trust in Jesus Christ. Concerning this access, Charles Spurgeon said:

> As soon as ever I have a vital connection with the Lamb of God, I am "in grace." Let me live on, let my grace grow, let my faith increase, let my zeal become warmer, let my love be more ardent, yet I shall not be more "in grace" than I was before. God will not love me more, he will not have a deeper and a purer affection in his heart to me then than he has the very first moment when I turn to him, nor will his grace the less justify me, or less accept me, the first moment when I come to him with all my sins about me, than it shall do when I stand before the throne.[40]

Ancient writers often used this expression about the grace of God: "to find grace in the sight of the Lord."[41] However, the New Testament never uses that wording to describe the Christian's standing of grace. It avoids this phrase because in the days of the apostles, it could have implied a moody, unpredictable god—one who was constantly angry and had to be soothed or found in the right mood. This wording might also imply that a person could never be sure about trusting God.

The Bible doesn't portray that kind of gruff, temperamental God. The position of grace and favor that is ours in Jesus is a *secure* standing place. Moffatt says concerning this aspect of God's grace:

> For him [Paul] grace was provided in the gospel by a God who had no moods or caprices; grace meant His characteristic, unvarying attitude towards men in need of help, it was favor to be accepted rather than sought out, favor that was offered freely to faith.[42]

We don't have to poke upward into a dark heaven and *hope* to find the grace of the Lord. On the contrary, His unmerited favor has already found us, and it must simply be received by a believing heart.

The last thing Satan wants to fight against is a Christian who truly understands God's grace and how to access it. So he lies to you and tries to discourage you from standing in it. He may try to convince you that God is moody, hot-headed, and probably irritated with you right now. Or he may try to tell you that you're just too sinful to even come before God. Satan has lots of experience as the accuser of the brethren (Rev. 12:10). Whether the lies are about God or about you, the answers against them all come in knowing the truth.

If the accuser tells you, "You're a sinner! You can't go before God!" The Christian can answer, "I know I'm a sinner, but I'm justified in Jesus" (as it says in Rom. 3:23-24). If he tells you your sin is too great or too horrible, tell him the greatness of Jesus' righteousness, because *that* is your standing! If he reminds you of your failures and backslidings, tell him you know all about them, but you also know a Savior who came to save sinners. Romans 5:2 means that your access to standing in God's grace can't be denied! Jesus paid the ultimate price to make sure you have a clear path to the throne of grace. Despite that, if you are tricked into thinking you don't have a right of access, then the privilege Jesus died to give will never benefit you.

Access into What?

It's encouraging to know that our access to God's grace can't be denied. But what good is it to come into that standing of grace? What benefits can we gain from our status of favor? First, notice that Paul wrote about *grace in which we stand*. We stand before God on the basis of grace and not any other basis. Not on the ground of our own works, whether they're past, present, or promised, and not on the principle of our own worthiness, even as God's children. If it weren't for grace, we wouldn't even *stand* before God—we'd grovel before Him. To "stand" conveys a measure of confidence, security, and boldness. Could you really stand before God if you came to Him on the basis of what *you* have done? At that moment, every sin you've ever even thought of committing would be made plain to you, forcing you down on your knees in humiliating submission before God. Thankfully, God has provided a better way to come into His presence. We come to the throne of the greatest King, and that's enough to make any of us tremble with fear. Yet the throne of this great King is a *throne of grace.*

Not only do we stand, but we also stand in *grace.* This means that God's attitude toward us is gracious and filled with favor. When God sees us, He's happy. He sees beauty in us because we're in Jesus. Standing in grace means that God *likes* us.

We've heard "God loves you" so many times that for many of us those words no longer have impact. We know we should believe it, yet it may be far more difficult to believe God *likes* us—that He's well pleased with us in Jesus. We often suffer under the thought that God barely tolerates us because we're unworthy, or that He's irritated with us most of the time. We're so familiar with our own sins and shortcomings that we're convinced God is half angry or disappointed in us. For those who *stand in grace*, their position before God is a standing of favor, acceptance, and beauty rather than unworthiness, irritation, and toleration.

Before patting yourself on the back, remember that your standing in grace has nothing to do with what you've done, what you are, or what you've promised to be. Your standing in grace is only because of God's freely given favor in Jesus. Though we may enjoy the privileges of a favored standing before God, we can't take the credit for that privileged standing.

We may also take comfort in the fact that God established this standing in grace as a permanent feature of our relationship with Him. God deals with His children on the basis of His grace, and it stays that way. Grace isn't grace if God withdraws it at a later date because of our lack of merit. We don't need to fear that He will one day find out how bad we really are and then put us out of His presence of favor. God grants us the blessings of His favor because of who He is, not because of who we are or what we promise to become. Therefore, we must stop trying to give God a reason to love us. So many Christians live their whole lives earnestly trying to prove themselves *worthy* of God's love. Yet, they're unable to receive that great love because *they're convinced they must produce a reason* for God to love them. The amazing thing is that God loved us first (1 John 4:19). Standing in grace means that all the reasons for His loving us are in Him and not in us.

Two Principles

God deals with Christians according to the principle of grace. In His eyes, we all stand before Him on the basis of unmerited favor. However, we may or may not choose to relate to Him by the same principle that He relates to us. God deals with all His children on the principle of grace, but we may choose to deal with Him either on the principle of law or grace (Paul eloquently makes the distinction in Gal. 4:21-5:1.). There's a great difference between the two systems, but the difference is found on our part, not God's part.

When we come to God by faith, trusting in Christ's merits and expecting love and blessing because of what Jesus did, that is grace. When we come to God by works, trusting in our merits and expecting only what we feel we've earned, that is law. This principle of law is familiar to most of us and is described by the phrase, You get what you deserve. If you're good, then God rewards you; if you're bad, He punishes you. God related to Israel by the system of law. In His covenant with Israel, God said they would be blessed when they obeyed and cursed when they disobeyed Him. Sadly, the biblical history of Israel saw the curses greatly outnumber the blessings.

The systems of law and grace cannot be reconciled with each other. Because they are opposite systems, we can't come to God on both principles at once, or even on a mixture of the two principles. They're different from each other at the very root.

- **Law** displays what is in *man* (sin); **grace** displays what is in *God* (love).

- **Law** speaks to us as members of the *old* creation, as people *stained* and *bound* by sin; **grace** makes us members of a *new* creation, *cleansing* the stains and *releasing* the chains of sin.

- **Law** *demands* righteousness from us; **grace** *brings* righteousness to us.

- **Law** sentences a living man to *death*; **grace** brings a dead man to *life*.

- **Law** speaks of what *we must do* for God; **grace** tells of what *Jesus has done* for us.

- **Law** gives us a *knowledge* of sin; **grace** *puts away* our sin.

- **Law** brings God *out to us*; **grace** brings *us in to* God.

Because of these contrasts, the principles of law and grace don't mix together. Lewis Chafer highlights the distinction between the two systems when he says:

> The Law of Moses presents a covenant of works to be wrought in the energy of the flesh; the teachings of grace present a covenant of faith to be wrought in the energy of the Spirit.[43]

These two systems stand as opposed to each other as the flesh is to the Spirit, as opposed as life is to death, and as opposed as God is to sin.

If we're not to deal with God on the basis of law, does that mean that the Law is evil or bad? Isn't there anything good we can say about the Law? The Bible tells us that the Law itself is good, holy, and just. It has an important place in the plan of God because the Law reveals the character of God and His holy standard. It performs a valuable function by clearly (and painfully) pointing out our shortcomings and our rebellion against God's standard. But as a principle to govern our relationship with God, the Law no longer has any place in His plan.

Rejecting Grace

When out of habit or out of choice we shy away from dealing

with God on the basis of grace, we automatically embrace the other principle of dealing with God—the principle of law. Connecting to the principle of law is the root of a graceless Christian life. If we forsake the new covenant and desire to relate to God on the basis of what we *deserve*, the results are disastrous. Many problems in the Christian life trace back to failing to *stand* with God on the basis of grace. We can know if we're living a life of law instead of grace by looking at a brief profile of the graceless Christian life.

Graceless Christians live with a perpetual cloud of guilt, never certain that they have *enough* devotion and good works to truly please God. They desperately want to please Him and do what's right, but because they believe that God's opinion of them is based on their performance, their minds are rarely at ease. They always feel the pressure of being under the watchful eye of a God who's ready to punish them at the first sign of disobedience. Christians who live by the Law never find lasting rest in the Lord.

Legend has it that in the early days of aviation, air travel was a dangerous novelty. One of those pioneering pilots offered to give an old man a birthday plane ride over the little West Virginia town where he had spent all of his 75 years.

The old man accepted the offer, and after circling over the town for 20 minutes, he was back on the ground. Of course, his friends asked, "Were you scared?"

"No-ooo," was his hesitant answer. Then he added: "But I never did put my full weight down."

Many Christians who live under law have the same hesitancy to really trust God. They have a hard time relaxing in His presence, and they find it difficult to sit down and enjoy what He wants to give. Instead of experiencing righteousness, peace, and joy in the Holy Spirit, their lives are marked by guilt, doubt, and fear that God will find out just how bad they really are and treat them as they deserve.

The greatest tragedy is that in almost every case, the law-living, graceless Christians have a genuine heart for the Lord. They have a sincere passion to please Him; yet they suffer under the haunting awareness that they don't measure up. What they want more than anything is to know God's love and acceptance, but they think this assurance of His favor will come through their performance. Grace says that the love and acceptance we long for from God is a gift given to us freely in Jesus. It's something we can't earn by who we are or what we do. Graceless Christianity is Satan's most subtle and damaging weapon against Christians who truly love God.

Christians who drift from grace and live under the Law often experience inconsistent victory over sin. This is because their eyes are frequently on themselves. Since they believe God's opinion of them depends on their actions, they analyze every thought, every word, and every deed in order that they might predict how God will treat them. This self-focused introspection takes away from the ability to rest and rely on the strength of the Lord. Without abiding in that power, we're unable to walk in the Spirit and find consistent victory. The self-focused Christian usually has the best intentions and wants to please God. Yet because of a graceless mindset, they're not focusing on Jesus, who reminds us that *"without Me, you can do nothing"* (John 15:5).

When the child of God who lives by law *does* experience victory, it can be even more dangerous because that victory tends to feed our pride. We begin to think we've conquered the monster of sin and made ourselves pleasing to God instead of seeing that Christ in us conquers sin and makes us pleasing to Him. When this happens, Satan catches his greatest prize—a saint who is sincere but acts self-righteously. Under law, our eyes are on ourselves and not on Jesus; this makes victory elusive, but dangerous when it's caught.

The Christian who lives under the Law might show little desire to get together with God or His people. There are two ways that an emphasis on law defeats the desire for Christian community. Law often makes a person say, "I'm not worthy, I don't belong." When someone feels like that, the last thing they want is the company of other Christians who seem so right with God that it makes them feel worse. On the other hand, a legalistic attitude may make a person think, *I'm the only one who's worthy in this bunch, and they don't belong.* An emphasis on their own performance for God makes them conceited. Nobody is holy enough or good enough for them. Either perspective reveals a graceless Christianity, and both work against the spirit of fellowship.

You can often tell a Christian who lives under law instead of grace when they strain for the approval of people because they're not confident of God's approval. Uncertainty of God's acceptance is a crippler. When we feel this way, we may try desperately to find approval from someone else. Once we get on the treadmill of living for the praise of man, it's difficult to get off. God wants to fill that need for approval within each one of us by dealing with us on the principle of grace.

Finally, believers who live under law may have a fear of failure in Christian service and a lack of boldness in their lives. They tend to fear failure because they believe that God's approval is on the line in everything they do. Reaching out to a person in need could be a good thing, but the Christian who lacks boldness fears that if they make a mistake, God will think badly of them. The law-living Christian may be afraid to do much of anything for God because they believe that they risk His displeasure if they serve Him poorly.

Fortunately, God doesn't deal with Christians on the basis of law, but according to the principle of His grace. The fact is, we *do* stand in grace before Him; He sees us in terms of favor, approval, and beauty, and because we stand in grace, we can expect blessing, not cursing, from God. Under law, blessings come from earning and deserving. Under grace, blessings come from believing and receiving. By His grace, God grants us undeserved, unconditional blessings. It's in response to those blessings that we do good works and seek diligently to serve and obey Jesus. Even when we do respond with obedience and devotion, those good works don't repay God for the blessings He gives, for the gift of grace never requires or expects repayment.

Doesn't God Get Angry with Us?

Most of us know how it feels to be disciplined by God, and we wonder if His discipline proves He does indeed sometimes get angry with us, or that He doesn't always deal with us according to grace. The chastening hand of God comes in different ways, but it's often some difficulty God places in our life to serve as a correction. Some people think this kind of "spiritual spanking" from our heavenly Father proves that He gets angry at us sometimes, and He gives us evil when we deserve it. But Hebrews 12:5-7 says we should regard the correcting hand of God as a special mark of His favor and kindness:

> *And you have forgotten the exhortation which speaks to you as to sons: "My son, do not despise the chastening of the Lord, nor be discouraged when you are rebuked by Him; for who the Lord loves He chastens, and scourges every son whom He receives." If you endure chastening, God deals with you as with sons; for what son is there whom a father does not chasten?*

Our heavenly Father is a perfect parent. As earthly parents, we know it's easy to discipline children in the wrong way, out of anger. This happens when a child irritates the parent. But God never corrects us out of irritation. As a perfect parent, He disciplines out of love. We may think God's chastening means He's angry or irritated with us, but it's only because we fail to see Him as the perfect Father who corrects us from a perfect love.

As every parent knows, loving correction is an important service to a child. Proverbs 13:24 says, "*He who spares his rod* [of correction] *hates his son, but he who loves him disciplines him promptly.*" When God chastens us, He gives His best when we may only want what's easiest. This is certainly a mark of His grace, even though at the time it may be painful or difficult. God, as a loving and perfect Father, corrects His children out of love and kindness, never out of anger or a desire to cause pain.

Making a Choice

As followers of Jesus, we're left with a choice. Our current standing before God is one of grace: He loves and accepts us apart from our own deserving or merits. The Father looks to the merits of

Jesus, not the merits of the Christian. We choose to relate to God either on the principle of law or the principle of grace. Will we agree with God and see ourselves as standing in grace, understanding that we must continue in grace throughout our Christian life? Or will we agree with the devil and the flesh and choose to see our standing before God in the principle of law? This choice affects every aspect of our Christian life. How can we make the right choice? Some concluding resolutions will help.

First, I must resolve to accept this favor of God because He's promised it. Remember that we have access by faith into this grace in which we stand (Rom. 5:2). God offers me a relationship of grace, and I must accept it by faith in Him, trusting His offer. I will cease from trying to earn God's favor and not wait until I feel worthy to receive His love.

Secondly, I must understand that because I stand in grace, I'm not on probation before God. Since my salvation or acceptance before Him is based on the merits of Jesus, I don't need to worry that God is waiting for me to fail so He can cast me away from His presence. Grace provides a secure, eternal standing for the child of God, one that He will forever uphold. I'm accepted in Christ; therefore, I'm fully accepted *right now*. If acceptance from God had to be gained through my merits, then it could only be granted after my performance had reached God's standard. But with grace, there's no testing period when God decides if He really wants me or not.

Thirdly, I resolve to regard God's chastening hand as a mark of His goodness and favor, not His anger and rejection. He only chastens those whom He loves.

Finally, I expect to be blessed by God on the basis of Jesus' merits. Because I stand in grace, I enjoy the favor and acceptance of my heavenly Father, and I expect that He will bless me, according to the riches of His grace.

Chapter Five

Accepted in the Beloved

*To the praise of the glory of His grace, by which He
made us accepted in the Beloved.* (Eph. 1:6)

Tennessee Williams, the famous American playwright, once decided to seek the services of a psychoanalyst. After several sessions, he suddenly announced that he would no longer speak with his therapist. Asked for his reason for this decision, he replied, "He was meddling too much in my private life."[44]

Apparently, behind Williams' humorous reply was a belief that little help could be gained from his time spent on an analyst's couch. Perhaps he shared the opinion of another man in the entertainment business, Samuel Goldwyn, who once said, "Anyone who goes to a psychiatrist should have his head examined!"[45]

Despite such opinions, many people today seek answers for their problems at the psychologist's door. Taken as a whole, today's psychology is a smorgasbord of ideas ranging from the sublime to the ridiculous. There's little agreement from one self-proclaimed expert to the next, and it seems there are as many different theories on what makes us tick as there are psychologists with loud voices or published papers. To the observing eye, it doesn't appear as though psychologists can speak with one voice on anything; however, they nearly all unite with amazing harmony on this fact of human socialization: we all have a vital need to feel accepted by others.

The need for acceptance is vividly displayed in our affection for stories about those who were once rejected but then received by their peers. For example, the circus elephant hero Dumbo was scorned and excluded by all the other circus animals because of his ungainly and ugly ears. No one accepted him for who he was, and He appeared doomed to a life of tears and rejection. However, by the end of the story, all the other animals accepted and even honored Dumbo because he had discovered his marvelous gift of flight. Those same floppy ears that had made him the object of scorn also made him admired and accepted by others.

Many of us hope to find acceptance and approval in a similar way. We think, *If only I could do something spectacular, then others would see that I'm a person of worth.* Often it seems like we're only one achievement away from truly knowing that others appreciate us. With the right accomplishment, we could earn their admiration and respect and have the wonderful assurance that we're accepted. Unfortunately, most of us lack the special powers to do something so spectacular, and we feel grounded in our own struggle to find approval and feel worthwhile.

What Makes Us Acceptable?

Society doesn't make our search for acceptance any easier because it has a cruel way of determining our worth. This rigid code of what makes a person valuable is preached on virtually every front. Television, magazines, newspapers, peer groups, and advertisers all join together in what seems to be a united conspiracy, telling us what's required if we're to be worth anything.

The number-one requirement for being accepted as a person of worth is physical attractiveness. Children who happen to be good-looking enjoy special status in school and around the neighborhood when compared to their less-attractive friends. Almost everyone knows what it's like to be laughed at because they look different, but for some people, this painful experience is a way of life.

Other standards for being a "somebody" in our culture include intelligence and wealth. If you're smart, or if people think you are, you can be admired even if you fail the attractiveness test. If you're wealthy, people accept you and consider you a worthwhile person because you have money. But if you're not beautiful, smart, or wealthy, you have three strikes against you. This is a cold, brutal system, but it's deeply ingrained in our society, and we must consciously deny these standards to think differently. The world's attitude toward social acceptance is the survival of the fittest; the beautiful, smart, and rich will succeed, and good luck to the rest. So if you ever feel like you don't measure up to this world's standards, take comfort—you're in the majority.

Fortunately, as Christians we don't have to take the world's standards as our own. We have God's Word to follow, and it offers a better way to determine worth and satisfy that great hunger for acceptance within us. If we embrace God's way of thinking, we must first deliberately and knowingly leave behind the thinking that marks our culture. We must make a conscious effort to pattern our values after what God says instead of what the majority says.

In his letter to the Ephesians, Paul teaches about finding acceptance. In Ephesians 1:6, he describes "*the glory of His grace, by which He has made us accepted in the Beloved.*" Paul revealed two important principles in this passage. First, by grace God has made the believer accepted in Jesus Christ. Second, this grace is glorious, and this work of grace is meant to bring forth praise in us.

Feeling Unacceptable

Everyone has a different approach to dealing with their need for acceptance. Some deny this need by playing tough, but a need can't be satisfied by denying we have it. Pretending we're not thirsty doesn't satisfy our thirst! Playing the game of denial usually produces an insecure person with a tough facade. Everyone thinks that such an individual is well adjusted, but on the inside these pretenders sometimes feel like they're coming apart at the seams.

Whether or not we admit our need to feel accepted, most of us turn this need into feeling that we're unacceptable or worthless. We come to believe that if we don't feel accepted, it's because we're unacceptable people. Everyone experiences these feelings of inferiority from time to time, but for many, these feelings of inadequacy, a lack of confidence, and a certainty of worthlessness are a way of life. Such people are often troubled by the thought: *My friends wouldn't like me if they really knew me.* This desperation is expressed by an old children's rhyme:

> Nobody loves me, everybody hates me;
> I think I'll go eat worms
> Little bitty tiny ones, big fat slimy ones
> Oh, how they wiggle and they squirm![46]

We become convinced the problem is in us, thinking that if we were the kind of people we should be, our need for acceptance would be satisfied. This produces guilt over a desire that God built into us for a reason. We blame ourselves for something that actually has a glorious, divine purpose—like hating ourselves for feeling hungry or thirsty. Rather than blame ourselves for a desire God has placed within us, we should instead go about fulfilling the need in the manner He has intended. Unfortunately, most people ignore God's way of meeting this hunger, and they attempt to fill it another way.

Searching for Approval

The Greek philosopher Diogenes once stood near a statue and begged for money from the sculpture. Someone noticed and asked why he was doing such a useless thing, and He replied, "I am practicing the art of being rejected."[47]

That may be fine for an ancient Greek philosopher, but our society today is given over to exercising the art of being accepted.

When we set out to meet our need for acceptance, we usually try to do it by the world's formula. We seek to make ourselves as attractive as possible, as witty and clever as we can be, and as wealthy as we can appear.

A woman starves herself on her diet, slaves over her hair and make-up, and then spends a bundle on clothes and jewelry. A man invests his time and money into the health club so he can have the right physique. People search online and in social media so they can say the right thing about current events or have a witty remark at hand. Things are bought for no other reason than to impress others. We do these things because we long to feel accepted by others, and we're convinced that beauty, intelligence, and wealth will pave the way. We desperately try to meet that God-given need for acceptance, but we're doing it the wrong way.

Our search for beauty or wealth isn't wrong or harmful, but as a means to answer our need for acceptance, it's completely ineffective. We soon learn that it isn't enough to be attractive. Once we've made ourselves beautiful, we then have to *stay* beautiful and wage war against the inevitable process of aging. Even if we feel that we've made ourselves attractive enough, we must endure those who accept us only because we're attractive. The same goes with trying to find acceptance by any of the world's methods. Tragically, we're not beautiful forever. There's always someone who is smarter or someone who has more of the right things that impress others. Hopefully, we'll soon discover the vanity of trying to find worth and acceptance according to society's standards, and we'll stop playing the world's game by the world's rules.

The need for acceptance is such a universal and stubborn drive among humans, and it's reasonable to see that God has placed this need within each one of us. We know God has given everyone desires that relate to the physical body (such as sleep and hunger), but sometimes we don't realize that He's placed emotional desires within us too. It follows that if He's placed this need in us, He has a divinely appointed way of meeting that need. Our physical bodies hunger and thirst, and God appointed that those desires be fulfilled with food and drink. But what about our need to be accepted by others? How has God appointed this need to be fulfilled?

God has chosen to meet our need for acceptance by entering into a relationship with us, whereby we receive His grace to satisfy that need. We were created to need other people as well, but the foundation of acceptance must be settled in God alone.

Highly Favored by Grace

In one sense, grace can be described as God's attitude toward us. It defines what God thinks of the Christian, how He feels about us in light of what Jesus has done. Our position on the basis of grace can be expressed like this: we are *highly favored* in Jesus, and never grudgingly accepted.

In the original language of the New Testament, the word Paul used for *accepted* in Ephesians 1:6 is *charito*. This word is only used twice in the New Testament, and the second place it appears is Luke 1:28. In that passage, the angel Gabriel comes to Mary to tell her she's been chosen to be the mother of the Messiah. This was a unique and special blessing, something that made her the most privileged person that had ever lived. When Gabriel appeared to Mary, his first words were *"Rejoice, highly favored one! The Lord is with you"* (Luke 1:28). The phrase *highly favored one* translates the word *charito* from the original language of the New Testament. Gabriel told Mary that she was highly favored, or full of grace, in the sight of God,

The apostle Paul used this same word *charito* in reference to how God sees the believer in Jesus. In other words, as special and blessed as Mary was—that's how we are to God. He sees us as highly favored ones, as acceptable to Him as Mary. It's difficult to think of any human who could be as special and blessed by God as the mother of Jesus, but Paul tells us that in Jesus, the believer is seen the same way. This shouldn't lower our perception of Mary, but it should lift *up* our perception of who we are in Jesus.

The fact that we're highly favored tells us something else about God's attitude toward us. It proves that He doesn't accept us reluctantly or with hesitation; He accepts us enthusiastically and joyfully. We all know what it's like to be accepted grudgingly. If you were ever the last one chosen when picking teams for schoolyard games, you know the feeling. The others may have let you play, but you were painfully aware that they didn't really want you on their team. The only reason you were accepted is because they knew that everyone had to be on a team.

God's choosing isn't like this at all. His attitude isn't *Well, I don't really want to accept so-and-so, but I guess I have to because they're in Jesus Christ.* The Father doesn't accept us with reservations or with lingering doubts. We should enjoy this highly favored status from the moment we genuinely trust in Jesus for salvation and living.

Indeed, Mary found this favor before God and was blessed with being the one who would bear Jesus. This privilege proved she was truly accepted by God. He would not give the right to bear His Son to someone who wasn't approved in His sight. The Christ child within her was positive proof that she was accepted by God.

Even so, the believer is also a bearer of Christ—not in the same way Mary was, but in a marvelous way nonetheless. Paul, in Colossians 1:27, spoke of this rich mystery: "*Christ in you, the hope of glory.*" Christ indwells the believer, and the believer is, in this sense, a bearer of Christ. Being full of Christ, we are also full of grace, even as Mary was. This privilege is evidence that we've been *completely* accepted by God.

What Makes Us Acceptable?

Why does God accept those who come to Him by faith, trusting in who Jesus is and what He did on the cross? Why does He see us in such terms of favor and privilege? According to Paul in Ephesians 1:6, there's only one answer: It's God's work, on the basis of grace, that makes us favored and acceptable in His eyes. When He accepts us by His grace, He accepts us on a principle that has nothing to do with what we deserve. He receives us because of the kind of God He is, not because of the kind of people we are.

Grace is the only basis by which we find acceptance before God. None of us can be good enough or do enough good deeds to persuade God to accept us on the basis of our works or merits. Our merits have no prevailing power with God, but the merits of Christ do have power. Jesus pleased the Father perfectly. He said, "*The Father has not left Me alone, for I always do those things that please Him*" (John 8:29). No other person could make such a statement! No one else has ever pleased the Father perfectly the way Jesus did.

Therefore, an incredible privilege is given to those who have not always done those things that please Him—to come before God on the basis of the merits of the One who has *always* pleased the Father.

There's a great deal of talk today about accepting Jesus Christ, and it's something that should be talked about. It's good to find out if others have accepted Him, but a more important question is this: Has God accepted you? The only way to find this status of acceptance and approval before Him is to look to the merits of His Son, trusting that the work of Christ at Calvary was completely effective in paving a way to God.

We also know that as Christians, we come before God in Jesus' name, not in our own. For example, if I went to Chase Manhattan Bank in New York and tried to withdraw $100, the teller would say, "I'm sorry, sir, we can't give you any money. You have no money deposited at this bank." My name would mean nothing to the people at Chase Manhattan Bank.

But what if I returned to the bank with a check for $1000, written by the largest depositor at the bank? The teller wouldn't care if I had money in that bank or in any other bank; she'd give me the money because of the one who signed the check.

Coming to God in Jesus' name is just like this. We have no credit in heaven in our own name, but when we come in Jesus' name and merits, we find the Father always ready to receive us and give us what we need.

When we come to the throne of God, we must come with confidence in the merits of Jesus. Whatever merits we may think we have will not be accepted. But Jesus was completely accepted by the Father, and because of God's generous offer, we may share in that acceptance by faith. That's why Paul says in Ephesians 1:6 that we are "accepted in the Beloved." The Beloved is Jesus, and we find our acceptance before God because of who we are in Him. God's favor is given on the basis of grace, in view of who you are in Jesus right now and not in view of works or good deeds that you might one day perform.

Breaking an Addiction to the Approval of Others

One of the healthiest things we can do is to become convinced that God accepts us fully and completely on the basis of who we are in Jesus. Indeed, He sees us in terms of highest favor. One great benefit we gain from this realization is that it satisfies the root of our need for acceptance. God created us with a hunger for approval, and He intended for it to be fulfilled in this manner. Knowing that the sovereign God of the universe accepts us is big enough to dominate our consciousness, and this knowledge should fill our lives with a security and peace that can't be matched.

When this root need is satisfied, we're able to get off the treadmill of addiction to the approval of others. This addiction to approval is poisonous. It makes us slaves to the crowd's opinion in even the small details of life. We seek to win the world's approval by playing according to their rules, and we end up being either frustrated and lonely or conceited and popular. Of course, it's pleasant to have the approval of others, but when we rest in God's grace, we can know that if others reject us, it's not because we're "unacceptable" people. If God accepts us, we're acceptable no matter what others say!

We must recognize that others won't always appreciate the beauty God sees in us. However, we can't begin to agree with those who don't see our beauty in Jesus and disagree with God.

In 1796, soldiers hostile to the Christianity and the church used the chapel of a convent in Milan, Italy for storage, sleeping, and later as a prison. They didn't think much of the paintings on the wall, so the threw stones at it and scratched out the eyes of some of the painted figures. The painting they tried to ruin wasn't a common work of art – it was Leonardo da Vinci's masterpiece "The Last Supper."[48]

How could anyone be so insensitive to a work of such beauty, painted by a great master? Despite the fact that those soldiers failed to appreciate Leonardo's genius, we know he was still a master artist. In the same way, even if others don't appreciate the beauty and favor that's ours in Jesus, we have it just the same.

What about Accepting Ourselves?

Our need for acceptance drives us to seek approval not only from others, but also from ourselves. Many of us have a more difficult time finding peace with ourselves than others seem to have in accepting us. People often feel as though they can forgive others, but they can't forgive or accept themselves.

Grace helps us deal with our need to be accepted by others, and it is also God's way of helping us accept ourselves. When we truly believe God's principles of grace, we can overcome the dark specter within that refuses to rest at peace with who we are in Jesus. All the while, we remember that our acceptance is *in the Beloved*. The reasons for our acceptance are found in Jesus.

Often our inability to accept ourselves is rooted in an inner demand to earn acceptance before God. As long as we feel compelled to provide God a reason to love and accept us, we'll fall short of finding that love and acceptance. God wants us to stop trying to give Him reasons to love us, and start seeing that all the reasons are in His Son. Our acceptance is *in the Beloved*, not in ourselves. Knowing this, we can cease from trying to forgive ourselves and come to rest in God's truth of forgiveness and reconciliation. The work of Jesus on Calvary was completely pleasing and effective before God. His work provides all we need for our reconciliation and acceptance. There's nothing we can add to His work to make it more effective. Finally, we can stop waiting to feel forgiven and begin believing God's Word and responding to His promises in faith.

Benefits of Being Highly Favored

When we rest in the merits of Jesus to meet our need for acceptance, we can know that we're fully accepted by God and we aren't on probation before Him. He isn't waiting for further evidence from us, because our acceptance is rooted in who we are in Christ. We don't have to live in fear that God will one day find us out or change His mind, leaving us outside of His love and favor.

Accepted in the Beloved means we can be free from the devil's deceptions that cause guilt. One of his great strategies is to convince us that God is usually irritated or angry at us, or that He's no longer our friend and has become our adversary. The devil tells us things like, "God's mad at you because you didn't pray today, and that's why some horrible thing will happen to you." When we put our faith in God's truth, we know this accusation simply isn't true. God certainly desires obedience and devotion from us, but He looks for these things after the issue of acceptance has been settled. To preach obedience and devotion first and acceptance in Jesus second is to put the cart before the horse. The cart and the horse go together (and in this case, they can't be separated), but first things must be placed first.

Settling the issue of our acceptance as human beings brings tremendous freedom. It means being rejected by another person is not the end of the world. Jesus told us that in this world we will face rejection and persecution, even from our closest friends and family. But when we know we're accepted in Christ, we don't live in fear of rejection by others. It may hurt when they exclude us, but it's a passing reaction. Instead, we find freedom to love and be who we are in Christ before the world because the issue of acceptance is forever settled. We know what God thinks about us, and that is enough.

Finally, believing we are accepted in the Beloved gives a correct view of self that gives God the glory. It doesn't gloss over the fact that apart from Jesus, we're destined for the judgment of God. It doesn't wink at the knowledge that without Christ, we're rebels against God, and that sin comes from us as naturally as breath. But as we entrust our lives to Christ and seek to be found in Him, it's a different story. The Father sees us according to who we are in His Son. We can take no credit for the fact that we're accepted in the Beloved, and we can take no glory for such a favored status before His throne. God alone gets the glory.

Why God Did It This Way

One of the overriding intentions of God in this plan is that we could see and praise the glory of His grace. When Paul wrote about *"the glory of His grace"* in Ephesians 1:6, he meant that God's glory and His grace go together. The glory of God is certainly a majestic topic that goes beyond human definition; however, it's helpful to understand His glory as being His essential nature. Glory is what identifies God as God. It includes the ideas of beauty, majesty, and splendor as well as greatness, might, and eternity.

Grace declares God's glory through His redemption and reconciliation of mankind to a position of "highly favored." Redemption and reconciliation coming by grace reveal the beauty of God's love, the majesty of His character, the splendor of His forgiveness, the greatness of His sacrifice, the might of His righteousness, and the eternity of His knowledge. In short, God's working of grace displays His glory.

This glorious grace was meant to bring forth a response in us. Paul calls us to *the praise of the glory of His grace.* It is God's desire that when grace works in us, it will stir within us praise to God. And under grace, God is praised because He's the one who meets man's great need for acceptance. No other person or thing can fill this need adequately. Under grace, God receives the praise for meeting our need. To be proud of our status as "highly favored" in Jesus is to be blind. Reflecting on this verse, Welsh minister D. Martyn Lloyd-Jones said, "Why am I what I am as a Christian? There is only one answer, I have been 'highly favored' by the grace of God. I give Him all the glory!"[49]

Those who are most familiar with the work of God's grace should be His most sincere, passionate worshippers. They understand how God has demonstrated His glory through His grace.

Don't Wait to Receive

In the days when the Western Hemisphere was truly the New World, exploring in the great ships was an occupation filled with danger. One constant problem was how to keep enough fresh water on board. Many crews died of thirst when stranded in a sea of undrinkable salt water.

One such crew was off the Eastern coast of South America, and they were nearly destroyed by dehydration. Their pleas for help were answered when, off in the distance, they saw another ship coming toward them. When the thirsty sailors pleaded for water, the men on the other ship told them to simply put down their buckets where they were! This seemed like a cruel joke. They were far out at sea, and land was nowhere to be seen. They knew that saltwater was deadly and that it could provide no relief to a thirsty man. But unknown to the parched sailors, the great Amazon River emptied into their waters and pushed out drinkable fresh water up to a mile past the coastline. They really could put down their buckets right where they were and drink the fresh water of the Amazon River. But instead, they almost died of thirst while sailing in fresh, drinkable waters.[50]

To each one of us who are thirsting to meet our need for acceptance, God says, "Put your buckets down right where you are." We don't have to climb a mountain or make a pilgrimage to find acceptance with God. We can simply come to Him with a genuine willingness to deny ourselves and trust in Christ completely. Satisfying our need for acceptance isn't far away; it's available right where we are. Do exactly what Martin Luther counseled his readers to do:

> Train your conscience to believe that God approves of you. Fight it out with doubt. Gain assurance through the Word of God. Say: "I am all right with God. I have the Holy Ghost. Christ, in whom I do believe, makes me worthy. I gladly hear, read, sing, and write of Him. I would like nothing better than that Christ's Gospel be known throughout the world and that many, many be brought to faith in Him."[51]

Chapter Six

Grace, Law, and Sin (Part 1)

Moreover, the law entered that the offense might abound. But where sin abounded, grace abounded much more, so that as sin reigned in death, even so grace might reign through righteousness to eternal life through Jesus Christ our Lord. (Rom. 5:20-21)

God's kingdom is not a democracy. He doesn't come to policy decisions by first discussing them with a congress of the angels or the company of the redeemed. God is the boss, He determines policy and procedure, and He does this without apology. That, in part, is what it means to be the sovereign God. Thankfully, it's a benevolent dictatorship with a perfect, loving Lord dictating the policies.

But picture for a moment an imaginary council in an imaginary "democratic" heaven. Pretend that God is explaining His plan for the salvation of man to the angels, and He tells them He will accomplish this plan by showing His love and favor to human beings—grace to be received on the basis of their faith in Him, not their behavior. He says it doesn't matter how much sin they have because He will offer more grace than their sin. And He explains that He won't motivate these redeemed ones by making them think they must earn His acceptance. Rather, He will love them so unconditionally that they'll obey Him out of gratitude.

I know that if I were one of the angels who heard such a plan, my mind would spin. Instantly I'd offer objections: First, if God dealt with these sinful humans on the basis of grace, they'd take advantage of Him and His grace. They'd sin intentionally, knowing they could always come back for more of His grace. I'd argue that if God wanted obedience from human beings, He'd better keep that threat of punishment over their heads. It would seem to me that grace was far too dangerous a system, and He should stick with the system of law.

We can all appreciate that the kingdom of God is not a democracy and that God doesn't depend upon the advice of angels. We also know that He's chosen to deal with man and offer him salvation on the basis of grace instead of law. However, aren't those objections still valid? Isn't it true that it's dangerous to say God grants His love and favor apart from our past, present, or future performance? Won't this open the door to living as we please and being unconcerned with God's standards?

You may know someone who lives like this. Their lives are marked by disobedience to God, but they believe that since God is so nice, He will let them off the hook. They may reflect an attitude that assumes, *The loving God will forgive my sins. That's His job!* They presume on God's grace and forgiveness but end up disgracing the name of Christ. Their unspoken motto is "I love to sin, and God loves to forgive. It's a beautiful arrangement."

From a purely human viewpoint, grace is dangerous. That's why many people don't teach or believe in grace, and they emphasize living by law instead. They believe if you tell people God loves and accepts them apart from what they deserve, they'll have no motivation to obey Him. In their opinion, people simply can't stay on the straight and narrow without a threat hanging over their heads.

Grace might be dangerous to us, but in God's plan He's made grace safe. He's implemented a system that effectively defuses the danger, and it's our duty to both understand and cooperate with that system.

In his letter to the Romans, chapters 5 and 6, the apostle Paul carefully explains the relation of God's grace to human sin. He tells how God has chosen to respond to man's sin in terms of grace, and how He's instituted a system which guards against the abuse of grace by those who receive it.

Abundant Sin, Super Abundant Grace

The way of the transgressor may be hard (Prov. 13:15), but it certainly isn't lonely, with no shortage of sin or sinners in the world today. A story is told of a certain radio preacher who announced that there were 572 different sins mentioned in the Bible. After his announcement, he received numerous requests for the list from people who thought they might be missing something!

Anyone who looks around can see that sin abounds in the world. Anyone who's honest knows that sin also abounds within. But what we may not realize is that the system of law *causes* sin to abound in us. This is contrary to the thinking of some people, who try to solve the problem of sin with the system of law. That is, they try to deal with sin by creating a long list of rules and regulations with the thought, *Do all these and then God will accept you.* But Paul tells us plainly and powerfully that instead of controlling and conquering sin, the system of law causes sin to increase.

How is this so? First, the Law clearly *reveals to us exactly what we've done wrong.* The system of law is like a mirror. If our face is dirty, we usually don't know how dirty it really is. We may think we look fine, but when we look into the mirror of law, we see exactly how dirty our face is. There's no escape from the knowledge of our sinfulness under the Law. This is one way that the Law causes sin to increase.

Another way the Law makes sin abound is that it *makes the offender to stand without any excuse.* Once we've seen the righteous standard of God's Law, we can't claim excuse of ignorance. Though it's true that ignorance of the Law isn't an excuse, it's also true that our guilt is much *greater* when we knowingly sin against God's revealed Law.

Also, once the Law is revealed, *it is rebelled against deliberately.* When we know what the rules are, there arises within us an impulse to break those rules. For example, once I was at a friend's house eating lunch. His food was on the plate, and his five-year-old son wanted some. But my friend solemnly warned his son, "Don't you touch my food!" When my friend turned away, his son almost immediately reached out his hand to touch the food. As he did this, he looked back at his father, but the father did nothing. The boy soon realized that his father didn't really mean it when he said, "Don't *touch* my food," but he actually meant, "Don't *eat* my food." When the boy realized this, he quickly tried to take a bite, and his father stopped *that* pretty fast! The interesting thing about the story is that this was not an especially naughty or strong-willed child. He was a normal boy and simply a fellow member of the human race. Whenever a standard is placed before us, a desire rises up inside to challenge that standard—an instinct that tells us to rebel against the command. This is one way that the system of law causes sin to abound. It prompts rebellion within us.

The place of law in the Christian life is important. We must be confronted by the Law and how it causes sin to abound in us before we can understand and receive God's abounding grace. If we don't realize that we're utterly lost in sin without Jesus, we'll have little appreciation of the great salvation He brings to us by His unmerited favor.

Grace can only be received and appreciated by those who understand that God owes them nothing but wrath. As long as we're unconvinced of our need for deliverance from the power of sin, we'll refuse to completely trust in God's grace for strength in the battle. Unfortunately, many people—even Christians—don't have much awareness of sin. Today when a preacher preaches against sin, he's likely to get a lot of nodding heads and vigorous amens. In generations past, the same preacher would likely hear the sobbing of those deeply pained by their own sinfulness and need for Christ. In the modern world, it's thought that sin is someone else's problem because *we* only make mistakes.

Fortunately, you don't have to plunge into a life of reckless sin to realize that sin abounds in your life. Whether you feel it or not, apart from Christ Jesus, you're plenty bad enough right now. The Holy Spirit can effectively reveal your sin; part of His ministry is to *"convict the world of sin, of righteousness and of judgment"* (John 16:8).

Like the direct ministry of the Holy Spirit, the Law is tremendously effective at showing us God's righteous standard and how far we fall short of it. The Law tells the bad news, but the good news is that God's grace far surpasses man's sin. Wherever sin abounds, God's grace can abound much more (Rom. 5:20). Paul's description of this grace in the original Greek of Romans 5:20 is especially striking—it essentially says that God's grace is "super-increased grace" or "super-duper grace."[52]

We'd never believe unless it was stated plainly in the Word of God. When we sin, God's response is to meet us with grace; that is, with His unmerited favor. By all logic, the judgment or anger of God should abound in response to our sin. Why does He choose to answer our sin with His grace? Has He decided to pass over His righteous judgment or wink at our sin? Not at all. He has responded to our sin with judgment and anger, but the glorious truth of the gospel is that God has already poured out that anger and judgment upon Jesus at Calvary instead of upon the one who believes. Therefore, when God responds to sin with grace, He's not neglecting His justice or righteousness. Grace can operate righteously because it works in view of the penalty Christ paid on the cross. Grace isn't God being "nice" to us, and it's not God merely letting us off easy. Rather, Jesus was nailed onto the cross for us and bore the wrath we deserved. Calvary stands as a permanent testimony to the fact that grace does not deny God's righteous requirement.

It's not only amazing that God responds to our sin with grace, it's also incredible that His grace abounds *more* than our sin. God has more grace than your sin (or the whole world's sin). There's absolutely no problem with the supply of God's grace. It's always available to us, and in measure that far surpasses our sin.

No one will be damned because their sin is beyond God's grace, but only because they refuse God's grace-filled offer of salvation in Jesus Christ. No one will be disqualified because of too much sin, but rather because of unbelief in God's gospel of grace. Ultimately, it's not sin itself that keeps us from God, because God's grace fully answers the sin problem of man in view of the cross. However, the love of sin does keep men and women from believing and receiving the good news of salvation. The grace of God can never be *exhausted*, but it can be *rejected*.

God's response of grace to my problem of sin means that the offer of cleansing He gives is available for me right now. There's no probationary period required because grace is received by faith and not by performance. If I come to God trusting in Jesus and His work on the cross, I don't have to worry that perhaps I'm not good enough to receive His forgiveness. God doesn't have a wait-and-see attitude toward me. Because I'm trusting in Christ and He's dealing with me by grace, the issue of my sin has already been answered by the provision of His grace.

Because God has chosen to respond to our sin with a grace that surpasses sin, we can see that grace is God's weapon in this battle. When God set out to slay the great beast of sin, He used the system of law to trap the beast, but He made use of the system of grace to slay it. Augustine had it right when he said, "The law detects; grace alone conquers sin."[53] But here's the matter that raises controversy: There are many who say that grace is an ineffective weapon against sin. They will tell you that instead of conquering sin, grace actually encourages sin because it teaches that God accepts us on a principle that doesn't look to our performance. Is this true? Does the system of grace have a fatal flaw that ensures its abuse? Will we find sin active where grace rules?

The Reign of Grace

Paul anticipated just such a line of questioning when he wrote to the Romans in chapter 5. There, he teaches about the characteristics of two reigns—the reign of the principle of law and the reign of the principle of grace. Law's reign is characterized by sin (the Law caused sin to abound) and death (because sin results in death). We also understand that under the reign of law, sin and death have a dominion that is strong and certain. Death's certainty is painfully displayed by every cemetery and every gravestone. Its strength is illustrated by the continual failure of the system of law to constrain sin in the history of Israel. From the idolatry with the golden calf at Mt. Sinai to the sins of intermarriage in the days of Nehemiah, the Bible's record of Israel's history shows that the grip of sin was powerful under the system of law.

If the reign of law has distinctive characteristics, so does the reign of grace. Paul tells us plainly that the central feature of the rule of grace is righteousness. Grace reigns through righteousness; wherever grace is ruling, God's righteous standard will be respected. The legalist's fear is that the reign of grace will provide wicked hearts with a license to sin, but that fear is not shared in Scripture. Grace doesn't accommodate sin; grace faces it squarely and goes above sin in order to conquer it. Grace doesn't wink at unrighteousness; it confronts sin with the atonement at the cross and the victory won at the open tomb. Grace is no friend to sin; it is sin's sworn enemy. Thomas Brooks said:

> Fire and water may as well agree in the same vessel,
> as grace and sin in the same heart.[54]

Dietrich Bonhoeffer was a man who understood that the Christian life is a call to real discipleship, not merely a system of intellectual beliefs. He taught that the person who truly believes in a righteous God must also have a longing for personal righteousness and holiness. Bonhoeffer coined the phrase, "cheap grace,"[55] which describes the type of life that the shallow Christian lives.

There's a great deal I admire about Bonhoeffer, but I have a true dislike of that phrase, "cheap grace." I agree with his concept and principle, but *there's no such thing* as cheap grace. To use that phrase is like saying "cold fire" or "white black." In fact, cheap grace doesn't exist. Any grace that doesn't build a desire and a growing toward righteousness within the heart of the believer is not grace at all; it's a pseudo grace. It's false and counterfeit. Charles Spurgeon, the great English preacher, stated it this way:

> If you have a kind of grace which does not keep you chaste, and make your behavior decent; if you have a sort of grace which lets you cheat and lie, which allows you to take undue advantage in trade, away with such grace; it is the grace of the devil, but not the grace of God, and may you be saved from it.[56]

Or, in other words, the grace that does not change my behavior will not change my destiny.

Believers who live by grace are not sinless. Though righteousness reigns in their lives, it isn't yet an absolute reign. Sin must still be battled, but the difference is that the grace-filled believer is willing to war against sin and carry that battle on to its final resolution. Sin will hurt the one whose heart is filled with grace. Believers haven't made a peace treaty with unrighteousness, but they're willing to fight on until God calls the war to an end.

As the system of law was marked by sin and death, the reign of grace is marked by righteousness and eternal life. Paul tells us, *"Even so grace might reign through righteousness to eternal life"* (Rom. 5:21). Grace answers the Law's sin with righteousness and responds to the death that law brought by bringing in eternal life. We've seen that the reign of law, accompanied by sin and death, was a reign that was both strong and certain. But the reign of grace is stronger and more certain because it is through Jesus Christ. Jesus Himself administrates the reign of grace, so we can rest fully assured that its results are certain.

Paul shows us that where the system of grace is in charge, there will be righteousness. God made the system of grace safe; it will not be a system marked by sin and a disregard for His holy standard. But how does this work? What has God done to make the system of grace safe?

Paul met this issue head on in Romans chapter 6. But before we can fully understand the answer, we must have an accurate view of the problem. There's nothing dangerous about grace; it's plenty safe, but we're not. The problem isn't in making grace safe for us. What could be unsafe about God's unmerited favor? The problem is in making us safe for grace. We're the ones who need to be changed, not God's principle of grace. So what exactly does God do in the believer to make him or her safe for grace?

Making Us Safe for Grace

What shall we say then? Shall we continue in sin that grace may abound? Certainly not! How shall we who died to sin live any longer in it? Or do you not know that as many of us as were baptized into Christ Jesus were baptized into His death? Therefore we were buried with Him through baptism into death, that just as Christ was raised from the dead by the glory of the Father, even so we also should walk in newness of life. (Rom. 6:1-4)

Paul anticipated the argument that grace would give people the permission to sin without fear of penalty. He imagined these people thinking, *Well, if grace abounds when sin does, and if I want to know God's grace in its fullness, I may as well go out and live a life of sin so I can receive a lot of grace.* How did Paul respond to this reasoning? He essentially told them, "Certainly not! That isn't how God arranged the working of grace at all."

He then explained that the first thing God does to make the believer safe for grace is to cause that person who believes on Jesus Christ to spiritually die with Him and then be raised with Him. This point is worth our careful consideration. Paul is saying that God makes a genuine change in the life of the one who believes in Christ. This change occurs in the realm of the spirit, but it's no less real than if it happened in the material world. And so, in the spiritual realm, when Jesus died, the believer died with Him. And when Jesus rose from the dead, the believer rose with Him.

Previously in chapter 5, Paul told us that when Adam sinned, every human being sinned in him (Rom. 5:19). This is what makes every person a sinner, because we all sinned in Adam. Even as we participated when Adam sinned (and we confirm that participation by our individual acts of rebellion), so all believers acted in Christ's death, burial, and resurrection. If this truth seems vague and unreal, notice that God gives us a physical demonstration of it—water baptism. Baptism illustrates the death, burial, and resurrection that are ours as we're identified in Jesus. Just as a person is put under the water and raised up from it in baptism, the one who believes on Christ has been *put under* with Him in His death and *raised up* to new life as Jesus was.

This incredible truth has far-reaching applications. The application Paul stressed in order to show how we've been made safe for grace is this: If we've died to sin with Christ, then our relationship with sin is broken. Those who have died are no longer slaves subjected to sin. They've moved beyond, to a different relationship with sin. The dead no longer have to battle with temptation. A major event has changed everything about them, including their former relation to sin.

What was it that died to sin when Jesus died?" Paul tells us in verse Romans 6:6: "*Our old man was crucified with Him, that the body of sin might be done away with, that we should no longer be slaves of sin.*" The *old man* is the self that's patterned after Adam—that part of us that's deeply ingrained with the desire to rebel against God and His command. The system of law is unable to deal with the old man within us, for it can only show us the righteous standard of God. The Law tries to reform the old man, to get him to turn over a new leaf. However, the system of grace acknowledges that the old man can't be reformed. He must be put to death, and for the believer, the old man dies with Jesus.

If the old man is dead, why do believers still struggle with the desire to sin and rebel against God and His commandments? Didn't all of that die with Jesus at the cross? When we who have been born again examine our own lives, it becomes evident that we have two natures; we all experience the feeling that there are two "selves" within us. This can be illustrated with homely proverbs about white dogs and black dogs that fight in the inner man, or with the image an angel on one shoulder and a devil on the other, each trying to bring us to their side. How ever we picture it, this inner battle is known to all who try to live the Christian life. But where does this struggle between the two selves come from?

The Two Selves

To understand that, we must first recall what happens in the inner man when someone is born again. First, we know that when we're born again, the old man dies with Christ. There's no doubt about it; the old man, the self that is inherited from Adam, the part of us that's instinctively rebellious to God, is dead when we're converted. Just as surely as Jesus was dead when He was laid in the tomb; so it's also certain that the old man is dead within each one who is converted by the Spirit of God. In light of this, we can see why the Bible never emphasizes a need to *put* the old man to death; instead, we're told to *reckon* the old man dead. The old man *is* dead, and we must, by faith, simply reckon it to be so.

The glorious truth of what happens in the believer at conversion doesn't end with the death of the old man—it continues with the truth that a new man is born in every believer, patterned after Jesus. Paul is as certain of this as he is about the death of the old man:

> *Therefore we were buried with Him through baptism into death, that just as Christ was raised from the dead by the glory of the Father, even so we should walk in newness of life. For if we have been united together in the likeness of His death, certainly we also shall be in the likeness of His resurrection.* (Rom. 6:4-5)

When we're converted, a new nature is imparted to us, a nature in stark contrast with the old man. The old man rebelled against God by instinct, but the natural inclination of the new man is to love and obey God. In two of his letters, Paul carefully defined the character of *"the new man, which was created according to God, in righteousness and true holiness"* (Eph. 4:24), and *"the new man who is renewed in knowledge according to the image of Him who created him"* (Col. 3:10).

The new man bears the stamp and imprint of Jesus Christ, while the old man (who is dead and gone) bore the imprint of rebellious Adam. Because the new man is created within us, after the image of God, we become *"partakers of the divine nature"* (2 Peter 1:4).

It's important to remember that dying with Jesus is only part of the process. Certainly we died with Him, but that was to prepare us for the greater work of rising with Him. As 2 Timothy 2:11 says, *"This is a faithful saying: If we die with him, we will also live with him."* Life is the goal, and the death of the old man is only part of the process. The Christian life involves taking up the cross and dying with Christ, but those things aren't the goal, they're only on the path to resurrection life. Many Christians experience the first part of the equation, but miss out on the joy of life with the risen Christ. Jesus never intended this incomplete experience for the believer!

We now know two things—that the old man patterned after Adam is dead, and the new man patterned after Jesus Christ is within us. But we also know that there's a struggle within us between two selves that seem to contradict each other. If the old man is really dead and the new man is really alive, why is there such a battle within?

This introduces the topic of the flesh, which is distinct from the old man and the new man. The flesh has many aspects, including bodily desires and habits. Our flesh responds to the influence exerted by the inner man, whether it's the old nature or the new nature. Although the flesh is morally neutral, it is under the destructive influence of the old man in each one of us. The old man engraves its imprint upon our flesh, upon our personality and habits. This imprint influences us for years, before we actually trusted in Jesus, and those years have taken their toll on us. The old man rigidly trained the flesh after his own nature. Even though the old man is dead and gone in the believer's life, his legacy lives on through the flesh, which is etched with habits and patterns of behavior that the old man found comfortable.

This is why the flesh is dangerous and why it battles with the new man for dominion:

I say then: Walk in the Spirit, and you shall not fulfill the lust of the flesh. For the flesh lusts against the Spirit, and the Spirit against the flesh; and these things are contrary to one another, so that you do not do the things that you wish. (Gal. 5:16-17)

The battle between the two "selves" in the believer isn't between the old man and the new man; it's between the new man and the flesh, which has been trained by the old man. How then can we find victory in this battle between the new man and the flesh? First, we must *deal with the flesh* the same way God dealt with the old man. Paul said in Romans 6 that the old man was crucified with Christ, and he also tells us in Galatians 5:24 that "*those who are Christ's have crucified the flesh with its passions and desires.*"

The old man is taken care of by the sovereign work of God when one believes on Jesus. But the job of dealing with the flesh is work that the believer is called by God to participate in through a decision of the will. The key to this battle is bringing the flesh and its desires under the power of the cross and in submission to the new man, patterned after Christ. When the flesh isn't under the authority of the Christian, it can influence us much the same way that the old man did, because the flesh bears the imprint of the old man.

There are two other important truths to keep in mind as we consider the struggle between the new man and the flesh. First, we must remember that the *real self* is the new man. Even though the flesh can exert strong influence on us and may masquerade as the real self, we can stand firmly on the Word of God and say that it is not. The real self delights in God's will and His love, and our call is to place the rest of our being under the influence of the new man. In a sense, there aren't two natures in the believer because the real nature is singular and patterned after Jesus. But in the midst of the struggle between the flesh and the new man, it feels like there are two natures within us and that each one is equally legitimate. That may be the experience of our feelings, but we know by faith that the only legitimate nature within us is the one created according to God in righteousness and true holiness.

Secondly, we must remind ourselves that the struggle between the new man and the flesh is a difficult one. The flesh has been well trained by the old man, and deeply ingrained habits and patterns of thinking don't usually change overnight. When we commit ourselves to the battle of bringing the flesh into submission to the new man, we shouldn't deceive ourselves into thinking it will be a quick, easy fight. We must dedicate ourselves to perseverance through a long struggle, and not let the loss of a single battle convince us that the war can't be won.

The Result of It All

The end result of this struggle is explained in Romans 6:14: "*For sin shall not have dominion over you, for you are not under law but under grace.*" Paul describes how the system of law is ineffective in combatting sin and, in fact, causes sin to abound. The Law keeps us under the dominion of sin, but under grace we find liberation from the oppressive reign of unrighteousness. This is because under grace, the nature of sin within us is put to death, and we're set onto the path of new life with Jesus. So how is it that we've been made safe for grace? We've been made safe by this amazing process of dying with Christ and being raised with Him. Grace is only safe for the one who has been set free from the domination of sin, and that is what happens when a person is born again of the Spirit of God. The one who has died with Christ will not live under the domination of sin. This is what the apostle John was speaking of when he wrote:

> *No one who lives in him keeps on sinning. No one who continues to sin has either seen him or known him.... No one who is born of God will continue to sin, because God's seed remains in him; they cannot go on sinning, because he has been born of God.* (1 John 3:6, 3:9 NIV)

Believers still struggle with sin and go through seasons of desperate battle. We remember that the influence of the old man remains and is expressed through the flesh; however, the old tyranny of sin is forever broken.

Those who have been born again in Christ cannot be comfortable in any habitual sin, for they are constantly reminded that their "habitat" is now righteousness, not sin. This is the first and foremost way that Jesus makes us safe for grace: He so changes us by identification with His death and resurrection that our inclination is no longer toward sin, but toward righteousness.

Chapter Seven

Grace, Law, and Sin (Part 2)

What then? Shall we sin because we are not under law but under grace? Certainly not! (Rom. 6:15)

A New Master

What Paul wrote about in the first part of Romans chapter 6 may be either good news or bad news for the Christian. The good news is that it answers many questions for us theologically. The bad news is that it may raise a greater problem for us in practical living. All this talk about God changing us and changing our desires seems distant to the Christian who's in an intense battle with temptation and sin. How does the system of grace help in that daily struggle against unrighteousness?

This is the question Paul took up in the second part of chapter 6 in his letter to the Romans. Feeling that he'd dealt adequately with the issue of habitual sin (telling us that it's utterly incompatible with the one who has died and risen with Jesus), he then turns his attention toward the issue of occasional sin, or sin on a day-to-day basis. In essence, He asks, "*Shall we sin* (occasionally) *because we're not under law but under grace?*" The apostle anticipates conversing with someone who thinks that under the system of grace, it doesn't matter if we sin a bit here and there. Now Paul shows us that such thinking opposes God's work of grace in our lives:

Do you not know that to whom you present yourselves slaves to obey, you are that one's slaves whom you obey, whether of sin leading to death, or of obedience leading to righteousness? But God be thanked that though you were slaves of sin, yet you obeyed from the heart that form of doctrine to which you were delivered. And having been set free from sin, you became slaves of righteousness. (Rom. 6:16-18)

Paul explains here that believers have undergone a dramatic change in lordship. In fact, God has changed our master. We're no longer slaves of sin; instead, we're now slaves to righteousness. One of the best descriptions of what it meant to be a slave in New Testament times was written by the Greek scholar Kenneth Wuest in his commentary on Romans 6.

Though the ancient concept of slavery is far removed from our modern world, in Paul's day slavery was an everyday institution. Because there were several different types of slavery, the word Paul uses to describe our slavery to both sin and righteousness is very specific. According to Wuest, this particular ancient Greek word indicates "one born into a condition of slavery; one whose will is swallowed up in the will of another; who is bound to the master with bounds that only death can break; one who serves his master to the disregard of his own interests."[57]

Consider this point by point. According to the term Paul uses, these four things mark the kind of slavery described in Romans 6.

- One born into the condition of slavery.
- One whose will is swallowed up in the will of their master.
- One bound to their master with a bond that only death can break.
- One who serves their master to the disregard of their own interests.

These things are true of our slavery to sin. We're born into this slavery (as descendants of Adam), and our will is swallowed up in the desire to sin. Sin is natural for us. It's also our practice to serve sin without regard to our own best interest. Our bondage to sin is permanent and can only be broken by death (the death of the old man).

In the 1960 film, *Spartacus*, Kirk Douglas played the escaped slave named Spartacus, who led a brief but widespread slave rebellion in ancient Rome. At one point in the movie, Spartacus said, "Death is the only freedom a slave knows. That's why he is not afraid of it."[58]

In the same way, the only way we can be set free from our slavery to sin is by death—not the death of our entire being or person, but the death of the old man, spoken of in chapter 6. Once dead to sin, we can then walk in newness of life, a life no longer dominated by unrighteousness and its bondage.

The four characteristics of slavery mentioned above, that once marked the Christian's slavery to sin, should now mark our present slavery to righteousness. We're *born* into this service of righteousness—that's what the new birth is all about—and our will and desires are to be swallowed up in the desires of our new Master. We will serve God forever, because our new slavery can only be broken by death, and we have eternal life in Jesus. In our service of righteousness, we're called to put aside our own interests and desires. These four things used to be true about the way we served sin, but now they should mark the way we serve righteousness.

Talking about a change of masters makes a striking theory, but there are ways to break it down in practice. We've been *genuinely* and *officially* set free from the slavery to sin we once had, yet there are ways we can defeat that work by enslaving ourselves.

In the 14th century, two brothers fought for the right to rule over a dukedom in what is now Belgium. The elder brother's name was Raynald, but he was commonly called "Crassus," a Latin nickname meaning "the fat," for he was horribly obese. After a heated battle, Raynald's younger brother Edward led a successful revolt against him and assumed the title of duke over his lands. But instead of killing Raynald, Edward devised a curious imprisonment. He had a room in the castle built around Raynald, a room with only one door. The door wasn't locked, the windows weren't barred, and

Edward promised Raynald that he could regain his land and his title any time he wanted them. All he had to do was leave the room of his imprisonment. The obstacle to freedom was not in the doors or the windows, but in Raynald himself. Being grossly overweight, he couldn't fit through the door, even though it was near normal in size. All Raynald needed to do was to diet down to a smaller size and then walk out a free man, with all the benefits he'd had before his fall. However, his younger brother kept sending him an assortment of tasty foods, and Raynald's desire to be free never won out over his desire to eat. Some accused Duke Edward of being cruel to his older brother, but he simply replied, "My brother is not a prisoner. He may leave when he so wills." Raynald stayed in that room for ten years, until Edward himself was killed in battle.[59]

This story describes the painfully accurate experience of many Christians. Jesus has set them forever free, and they may walk in that freedom from sin whenever they choose. But because they keep yielding their bodily appetites to the service of sin, they live a life of defeat, discouragement, and imprisonment.

Unfortunately, because of unbelief, self-reliance, or ignorance, many Christians never live in the freedom Christ paid for on the cross. D. L. Moody used to speak of an elderly black woman in the South following the Civil War. As a former slave, she was confused about her status and asked:

> Now is I free, or been I not? When I go to my old master he says I ain't free, and when I go to my own people they say I is, and I don't know whether I'm free or not. Some people told me that Abraham Lincoln signed a proclamation, but master says he didn't; he didn't have any right to.[60]

Spiritually, that's' where many Christians are. They are, and have been, legally set free from their slavery to sin, yet they're unsure of that truth. And, of course, our old master is always trying to convince us that we're not truly free from his dominion. Instead of listening to our old master, we must do all we can to walk in the liberty for which Christ has set us free (Gal 5:1).

How can we keep from enslaving ourselves, now that Jesus has set us free? Paul tells us how in Romans 6:19:

> *For just as you presented your members [the parts of your body] as slaves of uncleanness, and of lawlessness leading to more lawlessness, so now present your members as slaves of righteousness for holiness.*

When we were under the dominion of sin, we gave the parts of our body over to sin. Our *eyes* led us into lust, our *tongues* spoke gossip and lies, and our *hands* committed theft and violence. Paul tells us that the secret to living free is to present our bodies to the service of our new master.

There's a powerful picture of this in the Old Testament. When Aaron and his sons were to be consecrated as God's priests (Lev. 3), part of the ceremony involved the application of sacrificial blood to their bodies. The blood of a ram was placed on their right ear, because they were now to use those ears to listen to God. Blood was also dabbed on their right hand and right foot, because those parts were now to be set aside for God's service. Even so, we should reckon that because our bodies were bought with the price of Jesus' sacrifice, His blood is on our ears, hands, and feet so that they might be set aside for His service. When we live as though our bodies belong to Jesus, we'll find more consistent victory over daily sin.

Jesus has set free from sin, but we must continually choose to serve God with every aspect of our being. We must make a daily decision to consider ourselves set apart unto Him in body, soul, and spirit. Making a choice is important because when we're indecisive, it's easier to drift back into sin by the power of habit.

In Romans 6:19, Paul shows us another principle that's important in our battle to serve our new master: lawlessness leads to more lawlessness, and righteousness leads to more righteousness. The battle to reject sin and serve righteousness is in part based on the principle of momentum, or the snowball effect. You've seen the scenes in cartoons where a little snowball starts rolling down a hill. As it travels down the slope, it gains size and speed. Having begun in a certain direction, it keeps speeding in that direction, continuing with greater force and power.

The same principle of momentum carries over into the battle against sin. Habits of failure and compromise are difficult to break because lawlessness leads to more lawlessness. Yet when we establish a pattern of victory, the momentum gained can help us sustain victory, because righteousness leads to more righteousness. As we grow in righteousness, there's a danger that we'll become self-confident and start boasting about how well we stand, and that's when we're ripe for a fall. Nevertheless, it's important to remember that the habits and patterns of living we establish and reinforce today will have an influence on our future behavior.

Paul wraps up chapter 6 in dramatic fashion:

> *But now having been set free from sin, and having become slaves of God, you have your fruit to holiness, and the end, everlasting life. For the wages of sin is death, but the gift of God is eternal life in Christ Jesus our Lord.* (Rom. 6:22-23)

This seems too good to be true. We're set free from sin! Paul emphatically declares in the past tense that we have been set free from this terrible slavery. This means we never have to live under the bondage of sin again! Can this be true? Sin seems so inevitable. I feel the struggle within me every day. I know others who have proudly deceived themselves into thinking they've achieved some level of sinless perfection. But I do know that as I rely on God, I can withstand the *next* temptation. The apostle John warned, "*If we say we have no sin, we deceive ourselves, and the truth is not in us*" (1 John 1:8). In practice, it's unattainable to live the rest of my days without sinning because the Bible tells us that genuine perfection must wait until the flesh is completely transformed by resurrection (1 John 3:2). Yet I know that as I rely on Jesus Christ and walk in His grace, the next temptation can be overcome, and that's the one I should concern myself with.

I also know that when I do sin, it isn't because God has devised a system in which I *must* sin. Rather, it's because I've failed to rely on Jesus and submit my members unto His service.

Finally, we see that when sin is our master, the paycheck is death. Many sinners serve sin diligently in order to receive their wages. But when God is our master, we serve Him without pay. Remember that whatever is given of grace is given freely and never as a payment for what we do. We don't deserve the gift of eternal life in Jesus Christ, but those outside of Christ truly do *earn* their wages of death. The gift of eternal life (unearned, but freely given) is promised to those who choose to serve God in Christ Jesus. By changing our master, we also change our pay scale. Satan has plenty of hired workers; God only has committed, willing servants. They will be richly rewarded but on a principle apart from what they deserve or have earned.

Are There Exceptions?

Paul tells us about the dramatic change that occurs in our lives as we believe in Jesus. He speaks of how God uses that change to make us safe for grace, and then how He changes our master so that the path to freedom from the habitual service of sin is available to us.

But what about a Christian who shows no evidence that his old life is dead and his new life is in Christ? Or the believer with no desire to stop serving sin and start serving Jesus? Aren't these people abusers of God's unmerited favor—the very ones we fear will bring discredit upon His system of grace? We must soberly consider these questions in light of the biblical evidence and ask, "Can such people truly be Christians?" Perhaps this is evidence of a counterfeit conversion. Such abusers of grace have never truly experienced God's grace unto salvation. Redpath explains:

> An unholy life is merely the evidence of an unchanged heart, and an unchanged heart is the evidence of an unsaved soul. What value is there in the kind of grace which makes us no different from what we were before? None at all.[61]

Not everyone who goes to church or takes the title of "Christian" has genuinely experienced the transforming grace of God. Jesus told us that even the kingdom community, from the outside, is made up of both *wheat and tares* (Matt. 13:24-30, 13:36-43). He said that the net of the kingdom would capture both good and bad fish (Matt. 13:47-50). Both of these parables illustrate that, at least externally, not all who claim to belong to the community of grace have truly received that grace. It's God's job to sort the wheat from the tares, to separate the good fish from the bad. Yet it should not surprise us that some will arise who claim to have received the grace of God, and yet they live a life empty of grace and its work.

It's always dangerous to judge another person's eternal status from our earth-bound viewpoint. Still, we must say that those who have received the God's grace will display changes because of that grace. The changes may not be especially dramatic, and they may not be instantaneous, yet they will be real nonetheless. Perhaps the greatest danger lies in a tendency to assure people of a salvation that they have not genuinely experienced.

The evidence of grace received is a changed heart, and that changed heart makes us safe for God's grace. The process of conversion transforms our heart habitat from sin to righteousness, and it changes our master so that a path is provided for victory over even occasional sin. Christians through the centuries have recognized this essential aspect of doctrine. In the original 42 articles of the Church of England, the 10th article states this truth with a beauty that only 16th-century English can express:

> *Of grace.* The grace of Christ or the holie Ghost by him geven, dothe take awaie the stonie harte, and geveth an harte of fleshe.[62]

The one who receives grace cannot remain unchanged. If a "stonie harte" that loves sin and shows no evidence of new life present, then there has yet to be a genuine conversion in that individual. As Charles Spurgeon once preached:

> Wherever the forgiveness of sin comes, there comes with it a turning from sin, a leaving of sin, a fresh view of sin, a different estimate of it; and the heart, that once had sought its own pleasure, now seeks

God's pleasure…. Change of heart accompanies the
forgiveness of sin; and wherever that change of heart
is given, there springs up in the renewed soul a deep
sense of gratitude to God.[63]

We must never forget that grace does more than initiate the
Christian life—it also guides us into maturity and obedience. Grace
saves us, but it also teaches us how to live. Paul wrote to Titus:

*For the grace of God that brings salvation has appeared
to all men, teaching us that, denying ungodliness and
worldly lusts, we should live soberly, righteously, and
godly in the present age, looking for the blessed hope
and glorious appearing of our great God and Savior
Jesus Christ.* (Titus 3:11-13)

The one who receives the salvation that grace brings will also
be willing to receive the instruction that grace brings. The lessons
grace teaches in righteous living last a lifetime, and the distinctive
mark of the believer is a vibrant willingness to learn those lessons.
If someone refuses to receive this instruction, can that person truly
belong to Jesus? Has such an individual truly received the salvation
that grace brings? It cannot be so.

Grace Reigns

Paul makes many striking statements in chapters 5 and 6 of
his letter to the Romans. We've seen that we can't out-sin the grace
of God. We've learned that the reign of the principle of grace is
marked by righteousness and is not a license to sin. We've come to
the understanding that God changes believers in two ways to make
them safe for grace. First, He causes those who believe on Christ
to spiritually die with Him and be raised to a new life with Him.
Secondly, He removes us from our slavery to sin and draws us to
become slaves to righteousness.

In John Bunyan's classic, *Pilgrim's Progress*, my favorite character
was Mr. Honest—a traveler along the way who saw many fellow
pilgrims. Some of them set out boldly and strongly but eventually

turned back. Others stumbled at the start but later finished in fine fashion. Some began full of faith but ended in doubt. And others came to greater assurance as they walked the road of a pilgrim. Mr. Honest knew a lot about this pilgrimage we call Christianity, and he summed up all his knowledge in his last words:

> Mr. Honest called for his friends, and said unto them "I die, but shall make no will. As for my honesty, it shall go with me".... When the day that he was to be gone was come, he addressed himself to go over the river. Now the river at that time overflowed the banks in some places, but Mr. Honest in his lifetime had spoken to one [man named] Good-conscience to meet him there, that which he also did, and lent him his hand, and so helped him over. The last words of Mr. Honest were, "Grace reigns!" So he left the world.[64]

Grace reigns! Do those words sum up your Christian life? Either grace will reign in us or sin will reign—which will it be? Grace does the work that the system of law could never do. We can now understand that grace is God's means for both cleansing our sin and leading us in the path of righteousness. Instead of providing a license to sin, grace provides a way of victory over both habitual and occasional sin. In the fourth stanza of his famous hymn, "Jesus Lover of My Soul," Charles Wesley wrote:

> Plenteous grace with Thee is found,
> Grace to cover all my sin;
> Let the healing streams abound,
> Make and keep me pure within.

Chapter Eight

Sufficient Grace

And lest I should be exalted above measure by the abundance of the revelations, a thorn in the flesh was given to me, a messenger of Satan to buffet me, lest I be exalted above measure. Concerning this thing I pleaded with the Lord three times that it might depart from me. And He said to me, "My grace is sufficient for you, for my strength is made perfect in weakness." Therefore most gladly I will rather boast in my infirmities, that the power of Christ may rest upon me. Therefore I take pleasure in infirmities, in reproaches, in needs, in persecutions, in distresses, for Christ's sake. For when I am weak, then I am strong. (2 Cor. 12:7-10)

Most people are skeptical when someone tells about their personal conversations with God. If you ever want to raise eyebrows at a social gathering, simply say, "God told me..." Many times this skepticism is justified, because what people report that God told them often sounds suspect in light of God's more certain revelation. For example, why does it seem that when people in prominent ministries declare God has spoken to them, it often has to do with the latest fundraising scheme? Several years ago, a noted evangelist reported that he had experienced a seven-hour conversation with God, largely on the topic of raising money for his ministry. Curiously, God was well aware of the latest marketing and fundraising techniques, and the evangelist wrote letters describing the visit to supporters to let them know that this particular plea for money was specially ordered by the Lord Himself. No wonder many people adopt a wait-and-see attitude whenever someone begins relating their special conversations with God.

In all the New Testament letters, there's only one case of a writer saying, "God told me this," and it's in 2 Corinthians 12:9. Therefore, what Paul tells us here deserves our special attention as a unique statement in the New Testament. This passage certainly isn't any more inspired than the rest of our Bible, but since it's different, it deserves close examination.

Perhaps the best place to start is with an understanding of the context of Paul's writing. Paul suffered from what he called an "infirmity" or a "thorn in the flesh." It greatly bothered him, because the word he used for the thorn actually described something like a tent peg. His thorn was more like a railroad spike than a thumbtack. We don't know exactly what caused Paul such pain and discomfort, and if you were to consult ten different commentators, you'd probably get ten different opinions of what bothered him. Some say it was his eyes, some say it was a debilitating injury or sickness, and others tell you it was a person who constantly made his life miserable. Exactly who or what it was isn't really important; the important thing is that God let it remain, and He had a reason for letting it remain. Instead of focusing on what it was, we should ask, "Why did God allow this troubling thorn to remain in Paul's life?"

The answer is simple, but it has far-reaching and important applications to our lives. God allowed this painful problem to stay in Paul's life to teach him about grace and sufficiency. We can summarize what He taught Paul with one principle: God's grace is sufficient, and in ourselves, we are not—apart from that grace.

Our Own Insufficiency

American culture has many peculiar characteristics, and one of the most prominent is our long-established cult of self-sufficiency.

Generally, Americans are taught to embrace a fierce independence, one that requires we rarely admit any need or lack that we cannot satisfy ourselves. We've elevated the self-made man beyond the position of cultural hero to the place of national god. Our motto is that we can make it and we are enough to do so.

This kind of self-sufficiency creates a great obstacle in bringing the modern man or woman to Jesus. From the world's perspective, Christianity is just a crutch for people who can't make it on their own. Sure, it's fine for the wimps, winos, weaklings, and weirdos of this world, but normal people don't need that religious stuff. Our cultural embrace of the self-made man often contradicts the truth of our insufficiency. God's truth is plain and speaks pointedly to the fact that if man will be approved before God, he can't do it with the resources found only in himself.

We're told in a thousand different ways that we can make it by ourselves and we should have a confident, optimistic outlook because of our great potential. Sadly, much of that confidence and optimism is based on flimsy evidence and willing self-deception.

When Marie Antoinette—the last queen of France before the French Revolution—came to Paris as a bride, not a single ragged or starving person was allowed to show their face on the streets where her procession passed. At the time, France was filled with discontent born of dire poverty, a discontent that would later be fanned into the flame of revolution. But Marie Antoinette was not to know anything about that, so the poor and starving of the city were swept into the side streets where she couldn't see them. They were kept there so she would think that all were happy and prosperous in the city of Paris. It wasn't until the bloody and violent revolution that she learned just how bad things were. By then, it was too late.[65]

In the same way, we may feel optimistic and confident while deliberately refusing to face the facts. This can be a dangerous self-deception, a pitiful game of make-believe that we welcome with open arms. We often *want* to be deceived about our true condition, because knowing the truth could take away our beautiful lie. Whenever we want to deny our need for God, there's always a satanic deceiver at hand to smoothly tell us what we long to hear. Instead of knowing the truth, many are satisfied with a facade of happiness and superficial answers to their deep spiritual needs. Turning a blind eye to our inherent weaknesses and insufficiencies is a shallow and tragic aspect of our character that could lead us to confidently deny our need for a Savior.

Jesus described this state of mind in Mark 2:17: *"Those who are well have no need of a physician, but those who are sick. I did not come to call the righteous, but sinners, to repentance."* As long as we think we're well and that only losers need Christ, then Jesus' call makes no difference to us. It's only when we become convinced of our own insufficiency that we will receive God's grace, which can truly be our sufficiency.

It's also important to recognize that we can only be convinced of our insufficiency by the Holy Spirit. We can't talk anyone into an understanding of their spiritual need apart from the Holy Spirit working in them. He must do the work of conviction and demonstration concerning the truth about a person's need. God may use others in this work, but the persuasive internal witness can be accomplished by His Spirit alone. One reason why many people have an insincere commitment is because they come to Jesus without being persuaded by the Holy Spirit of their great need for Him. If Jesus is seen as something good that's merely added to our lives, then we'll never have the relationship He intended to have with us.

God's Answer for Our Need

Once we've taken an honest look at our own insufficiency, we can then think about the way God wants to meet that need. He has ordained that His grace is fully sufficient. When we become aware of our spiritual need, then God calls us to a dependence on His grace.

Consider what a counselor without a biblical perspective would have said to Paul. Imagine Paul telling the counselor about his great infirmity, his troublesome thorn in the flesh, and how he felt weak and powerless to continue on. We might imagine the counselor saying, "Well, Paul, what you need is a positive mental outlook to meet this problem." Or "Paul, the power is within you to conquer this infirmity. You should look deep within the inner man to find the resources for success." Perhaps the counselor would then say, "What you really need is a support group of caring individuals." The counselor might even challenge Paul: "If you really had faith, you'd be delivered from this thorn in the flesh." Some of this advice might be helpful under different circumstances. Yet God had special counsel for Paul in this situation—different from most human answers.

How *did* God answer Paul? "*My grace* [unmerited favor] *is sufficient*" (2 Cor. 12:9). In other words, My grace is enough to meet your need, so look unto Me! God's plan wasn't for Paul to find the answer in himself, or even in other people (though others may have helped greatly). God's plan was that Paul's need would be satisfied by a touch of His grace.

How can God's grace be sufficient to meet our needs? Grace can meet our needs, because when we receive it, we enjoy our status of favor and approval in God's eyes. Grace means that God likes us— that He is favorably disposed toward us, we have His approval, and the promise of His care. We all know that being in good graces with an influential person can get us far along. It really is true that what you know isn't as important as who you know, and being in God's grace means that you know Him, and He knows and cares for you.

God's grace can meet our needs because it's available at all times. When we sin or fail, we're not outside the reach of His grace. Since grace is given freely to us in Christ, it can't be withdrawn at a later date if we stumble or fall. When we come to God by faith through the blood of Jesus, His grace is ever ready to meet and minister to our insufficiencies.

Finally, His grace can meet our needs because God told Paul that grace is the strength of God (2 Timothy 2:1). So much of the power of this world is expressed in things that bring harm and destruction, but God loves to show His power through His goodness and grace.

Sometimes we associate such a pure goodness with cowardice or timidity. But to take such a view is to agree with the world's perspective of power and strength, and to deny God's truth about the strength of grace and love. Grace isn't weak or wimpy; it's the very power of God to fulfill what's lacking in us.

We see then that when we're made aware of our own insufficiency, God's intention is to meet that need by the working of His unmerited favor and approval in our lives. He wants us to look to Him in those times of infirmity, not to ourselves or to what man can provide.

Of course, this doesn't mean we shouldn't turn to others when we're in need. If that were the case, the many encouragements in the Bible to care for each other and bear one another's burdens wouldn't make sense. Jesus wants to minister to us both directly and through others. We should never neglect to wait on God in our times of need, that we may directly receive from Him the grace to meet our need. Yet we also look for God's grace to meet us through others. Jesus loves to meet needs through His corporate body.

Instead of looking for answers in ourselves, we rest and rejoice in the assurance of His favor and approval. And we await the working of Jesus' hand of grace to strengthen us, either directly or through others He uses to help us.

A Life-Long Experience

2 Corinthians 12:7-10 also shows us that we will experience weakness and must rely on God's grace throughout our Christian life. Our progress will never cause us to grow beyond the need to rely on His grace. We'll never come to a place where we fail to experience that we're utterly insufficient apart from that working of grace. We're called to a constant reliance upon grace for our entire Christian experience.

Paul's own life displays a vivid example of this principle. We see that God brought weakness his way so he could learn to rely on the strength of God. Think about it—Paul, the great missionary and apostle, perhaps the most famous Christian in all history, was deliberately kept in some manner of weakness by God so he might never lose sight of his need to rely on Him. God knew Paul needed to experience weakness, so He made an occasion for Paul to experience that weakness through his infirmity or thorn in the flesh.

As believers, the experience of weakness is therefore a good thing, causing us to look beyond ourselves for the resources to walk the Christian way. We all need to experience this type of weakness so we will constantly seek our strength in God. However, I admit that at this point in my own Christian life, God doesn't have to do anything special to make me aware of my own insufficiencies, because I supply quite enough weakness all by myself.

God's reason for submitting Paul to this weakness wasn't to punish Paul or keep him in line or make him weak for the sake of keeping him weak. God doesn't take pleasure in such things. Rather, He knew Paul would only continue to experience the strength of God if he continued to also experience the weakness of man. God didn't try to defeat Paul. Rather, He made the way of victory through grace more available to him by revealing the weakness in himself.

That's why Paul could boast in his infirmities and take pleasure in his difficulties. He wasn't some sick person who enjoyed it when life caved in all around him. He only boasted in his infirmities because they were the way he could know the strength and victory of God's grace. It was the strength and victory that Paul cherished, and whatever God used to accomplish that victory, Paul bragged about it.

It's helpful to consider what kind of man Paul was. Was he weak man or a strong man? This one who traveled around the ancient world spreading the gospel of Jesus, despite the fiercest persecutions, who endured shipwrecks and imprisonments, who preached to kings and slaves, and who established strong churches and trained up their leaders was not a weak man. In light of his life and accomplishments, we would say Paul was a very strong man, but he was only strong because he knew his weaknesses and looked outside himself for the strength of God's grace. In the same way, if we're going to live lives of such strength, we also need to admit our weaknesses and look to God alone for the favor, approval, and work of grace that will strengthen us for any task. It was the grace-filled Paul who could say, *"I can do all things through Christ who strengthens me"* (Phil. 4:13).

Practical Applications

First, these truths will change how we pray for those who haven't received God's gift of grace unto salvation. In 2 Corinthians 4:4, Paul said that the minds of those who are perishing have been blinded by the god of this age, and they do not believe, lest the light of the gospel of the glory of Christ—who is the image of God—should shine on them. This blinding work of Satan has many different aspects, but surely one of the greatest is persuading men and women that they have no need for Jesus. We must battle against this work of deception with earnest prayer for the lost, that they may perceive their own weaknesses, insufficiencies, and their great need for the Savior.

We now understand that one of the very best prayers we can offer for those who don't know Jesus is this: *God, make them know their need for You and their utter weakness apart from You.* You may think it's a cruel thing to pray that another person would come to understand their own weakness, but they will never trust in the strong salvation of Jesus until they do. When we understand that it's often an attitude of self-sufficiency that keeps people from Christ, it will affect the way we pray for them.

Secondly, these truths change how we see success and growth in the Christian walk, not in terms of independence, but in a greater dependence. There's a longing within most of us for a day when the Christian life will become easy. We hope for a time when our major struggles with sin are behind us and we can go on to bigger and better things without much of a struggle. That day is an illusion. If the apostle Paul himself constantly experienced weakness, who are we to think that we'll go beyond him? Indeed, this section of Scripture shows us that if need be, God will bring something specific into our life to remind us of our weakness and great dependence on Him.

Finally, these truths warn us of the danger of pride, for it is the great enemy of grace and that makes us unwilling to see our weakness. To proudly deny our weakness and absolute need to depend on Jesus is true blindness and the ultimate arrogance. It's as if we're telling God, "Lord, most people may not have what it takes, but I do. I don't need Your offer of grace for strength and victory." Those who harbor such an attitude (though they may never voice it) are self-condemned because they openly reject God's provision for their need.

Paul couldn't have put it more clearly: God's grace is sufficient to meet the needs of mankind, and we are not sufficient to meet those needs in ourselves.

Chapter Nine

Working with Grace

For I am the least of the apostles, who am not worthy to be called an apostle, because I persecuted the church of God. But by the grace of God I am what I am, and His grace toward me was not in vain; but I labored more abundantly than they all, yet not I, but the grace of God which was with me. (1 Cor.15:9-10)

Some of the most profound statements by the apostle Paul were made as side comments while he addressed another subject. This passage from 1 Corinthians 15 is a perfect example. Paul's main focus in this chapter was not to teach about grace but to defend the essential Christian doctrine of the resurrection of the dead.

He did this by pointing out the obvious truth that the resurrection of Jesus proves the dead are raised. However, someone might object and ask, "How do we know that Jesus rose from the dead?" Paul had a ready reply. First, we know that Jesus rose from the dead because we have the reliable eyewitness testimony of the apostles to this fact. Peter, James, John, and all the rest of the apostles saw the resurrected Jesus, and they staked their lives on this testimony.

Along with the apostles, Paul added his own testimony to the truth of Jesus' resurrection. He also claimed to be an apostle and a fellow witness of the resurrected Christ. But who was he to claim such a high position? He didn't follow as the others did in the years of Jesus' earthly ministry. Jesus didn't call out to Paul on the shores of the Sea of Galilee and say, "Follow Me." Paul wasn't one of the 70 disciples commissioned to preach the gospel in the cities of Galilee. He didn't hear the Sermon on the Mount or Jesus' Upper Room Discourse with his own ears. Why did Paul think he could take the privileged title of *apostle* for himself?

Paul said one reason he could claim this status was because he also saw the resurrected Jesus. Acts chapter 9 describes Paul's personal encounter with Christ, but this event occurred long after the other apostles had seen their resurrected Lord. That's why Paul says he was like "*one born out of due time*" (1 Cor. 15:8). Yet simply seeing the resurrected Jesus was not enough to make someone an apostle. If it were, then there would have been more than 500 apostles in Paul's day, because we're told in 1 Corinthians 15:6 that there were more than 500 brethren who saw the risen Lord. What else could Paul say to justify his claim of being an apostle? What right did he have to claim such an important position? Paul told us that his transformation from terrible persecutor to honored apostle was due to one thing: the grace of God.

Changed by Grace

In this simple statement in 1 Corinthians 15:9-10, Paul gives us insight into one of the most remarkable aspects concerning the impact of God's grace upon human lives. Grace changes people, and it changes them in both unexpected and dramatic ways.

When we genuinely believe on Jesus and are converted by the Holy Spirit, there will always be a change of life. There can never be any doubt that "*if anyone is in Christ, he is a new creation; old things have passed away; behold all things have become new*" (2 Cor. 5:17). The changes may differ from person to person, but the changes are certain and expected. Something is wrong when a person says they've been born again, but there's no evidence of change in their fundamental beliefs, their perspective of life, or their attitude toward God and sin. Grace can't be given to someone without an evident change. God and His grace are not simply added to the lives of those who believe; rather, He becomes their focus and purpose. In everyone who genuinely believes, an individual work of transformation begins that touches every aspect of life.

Yet the power of grace is not only given to work an initial change in the life of the believer; it's given so that it will continue to change us. God wants His transforming power of grace to always be at work in the life of the Christian. Paul realized that God wasn't finished changing him and was willing to admit, *"Not that I have already attained, or am already perfected; but I press on, that I may lay hold of that which Christ Jesus has also laid hold of me"* (Phil. 3:12).

We should stop for a moment to consider just who wrote this letter and how remarkably the power of grace had changed his life. Before being confronted by God on the road to Damascus, Paul was religiously smug, but also a hater of God and His church. He felt that he had satisfied God's requirements, but according to God's standards, he was not righteous. In his self-righteous confidence, he lashed out against the early band of Christians, persecuting them more enthusiastically than any of his associates. Paul was sure God was on his side and was blessing his attempt to stamp out these followers of Jesus.

However, Paul was deeply deceived, because in persecuting God's church he actually persecuted Jesus Himself. Remember Jesus' words on the road to Damascus: *"Saul, Saul, why are you persecuting Me?"* (Acts 9:4). By hating the church, Paul displayed his hatred for Jesus, and his hatred for Jesus showed that Paul really hated the God of Israel. This is because Jesus is the exact representation of God the Father, the God that Paul supposedly served by attacking the church. Paul was so deceived that he saw himself as greatly pleasing to God when, in fact, his life displayed an intense hatred of the Father, Son, and Holy Spirit, as well as the church.

When we consider Paul's life before the Damascus road, we're amazed to see the change in him after his experience with Jesus. Paul's eyes were opened, both figuratively and literally, because the shining vision of Christ on the Damascus road left him blind until a believer named Ananias prayed for his healing. Once blind, Paul came to see that he had been deceived, and he came to realize that his previous life hadn't pleased God at all. Instead of persecuting the church, Paul humbly joined with other Christians, and instead of hating the gospel of Christ, he boldly preached it. Such a remarkable transformation was only possible through a work of God's grace. No psychological or biological phenomenon could account for such a change. All the glory and credit must be given to Jesus and His grace alone. Paul learned what being a new creation was all about, and he knew by his own experience the dramatic change that takes place when someone stops fighting against God and puts their trust in Jesus.

We all have a tendency to think that this type of real, dramatic change is confined to the dusty pages of ancient books, but that isn't true. The power of God's grace to change lives is for today, and it even works for people in dramatic rebellion against Him. One example of a Saul-to-Paul conversion is in the life of a man named Sergei Kourdakov, who wrote of his remarkable transformation in a book simply titled *Sergei*.

As a youth, Sergei led more than 150 attack gangs against Christians in the Soviet Union. Like a modern-day persecuting Saul of Tarsus, he tried to intimidate the believers of Russia by beating them without mercy, sometimes so severely that his unfortunate victims would die. On one occasion, he was shown on Soviet television wrapped in their national flag and described as the perfect example of Soviet youth. He had been completely brainwashed by atheistic philosophy and utterly deceived about the truth of God or Christianity.

One day God broke through to Sergei and proved that He was real. This happened as Sergei witnessed the character of Soviet believers, especially the way they prayed for those who persecuted them. He later joined the Soviet Navy, and eventually, in a desperate effort to escape to a place where he could learn the truth about God, he jumped ship in the icy Arctic Ocean near Canada and swam for more than eight hours to shore. After reaching safety, he immediately began to learn about the God he once hated. Sergei fasted for two days and spent all that time kneeling at an altar in a church, praying to a God he didn't know, until a pastor told him how to find what he was looking for in Jesus Christ. Sergei Kourdakov then preached the gospel he once tried to destroy, loving and serving the Savior he once bitterly hated.[66]

Sergei Kourdakov is another striking testimony to the fact that grace still changes lives. God didn't stop this work in the days of the Bible; He continues it to this day for anyone who will forsake all to follow Him. How about you? Have you been changed by the power of God's grace?

Working with Grace

When we consider the amazing life transformation in someone like Paul or Sergei Kourdakov, we may think that all they did was sit back and let the power of grace overwhelm them, but that isn't true. Because we know this work of change requires the active participation and effort of the one being changed.

Paul told us that God's grace was not extended to him *"in vain"* (1 Cor. 15:10). Paul also worked hard in concert with the grace of God. Grace didn't discourage him from working; it encouraged and strengthened him to work. The grace of God produced much fruit in Paul, in part because he acted on his desire to work alongside God's grace.

However, by saying *"His grace toward me was not in vain,"* Paul brings up an interesting question concerning the grace of God: Can it indeed be given in vain? Can God's grace be given and received, but have no effect in the life of the one who receives it?

To answer this question, we must remember that no works are required to receive grace; only faith is needed. Romans 5:1-2 says: *"We have peace with God through our Lord Jesus Christ, through whom we also have access by faith into this grace in which we stand."* Our access into grace is *by faith.* God gives this power of favor and acceptance we call grace without first requiring worth or merit. It's not given with a prerequisite of performance—not in the past, present, or future. However, God doesn't grant us this life-changing grace so that we might relax and refuse to couple our efforts with the power of His grace. God expects us to do many specific things with His grace, and several of these are clearly outlined in Scripture.

Grace for Obedience

For example, in Romans 1:5 we read, "*We have received grace... for obedience to the faith.*" This plainly tells us that part of God's purpose in giving us His grace is so we will obey Him, and God expects those who receive grace to be concerned with obedience. What about those who say they've received God's grace unto salvation yet they display no concern for obedience? Jude, in his short letter, described these as "*ungodly men, who turn the grace of our God into lewdness and deny the only Lord God and our Lord Jesus Christ*" (Jude 1:4). God says that such people are under His coming judgment "*who long ago were marked out for this condemnation*" (Jude 1:4). Such people prove they have never really received God's grace. Grace is given so that we might obey, and chronic disobedience and abuse of grace is evidence that one has never properly received the grace of God.

Grace for Good Works

In his second letter to the Corinthian church, Paul lists an additional reason that God gives us His unmerited favor. Paul wrote in 2 Corinthians 9:8, "*God is able to make all grace abound toward you, that you, always having all sufficiency in all things, have an abundance for every good work.*" God wants us to have all the resources necessary to do the good works He created us for. To do good works we may need boldness, a willing heart, finances, spiritual wisdom, or other resources. God's grace works in us to supply these needs so we can do good works. Yet with such a supply, we still must actually *do* the things that His grace enables us to do. Grace is given that we might do good works.

Grace for Serving God

Another thing God expects us to do with the grace we receive is to *serve* Him. In Hebrews 12:28, the writer says, *"Let us have grace, by which we may serve God acceptably with reverence and godly fear."* Grace helps us serve God in many different ways. It gives us the moral ability to serve in a way that's pleasing to Him, because under the system of grace, the sin problem of man is adequately addressed. Before the cleansing we received by way of the cross, the only service we could offer God was performed with sin-stained hands. God looks for servants who are washed before they serve Him, even as the Old Testament priests had to be ceremonially washed before performing their duties. God's plan of grace provides the way we can offer unstained service to God.

In addition, grace helps us serve God out of the right motivation. Apart from an awareness of grace, we will often serve God so we can feel accepted by Him. Through our works, we try to give Him a reason to love us. Grace assures us that all those reasons are in God and not in us, and that we are accepted in Jesus. Then our service is rightly motivated out of love, appreciation, and gratitude. We do want the reward of pleasing God, as a child loves to please their father, but not to *earn* God's approval.

An awareness of God's grace also helps us serve God well in one of the most important ways we can—worship. When the issue of our acceptance before God is settled by His unmerited favor, and there is true rest in the heart, then worship takes on an exciting new dimension, marked by intense thanksgiving and adoration for what God has done in our lives. In light of grace, we worship God out of gratitude, not out of trying to win His approval or soothe His anger. We aren't worried that God may reject us if we don't please Him, because by grace the issue of acceptance is forever settled by the work of Christ. With the fear of rejection removed, we can serve God in worship out of a joyful appreciation for all He's done for us. Grace is given so that we might serve God.

Grace for Serving Others

A fourth purpose for God giving His grace can be seen in Ephesians 3:7, where Paul tells us, "*I became a minister according to the gift of the grace of God.*" Grace was the basis of Paul's ministry, and he knew God had given him this grace so he would serve the body of Christ. Therefore, not only do we serve God with the resources of grace, but we're also able to serve the church with the same resources grace provides. In the same way, grace influences the way we serve the body of Christ. Our service comes from gratitude and love instead of guilt or fear of impending punishment if we happen to fail in our service. God gives us grace so we might minister to His church.

We see plainly that we receive grace to obey God, do good works, and serve Him and His church. However, we must realize that God doesn't give us grace because we do these things, but only so we will have the desire, ability, and resources to do them. Grace is never a reward for good deeds either done or promised; it's given so we might do the things that please God.

Partners with God

Paul understood that God gives us His grace and then we're equipped to labor abundantly. The result is that God's work is done. Results come when we realize we're in a partnership with God. It's difficult to understand why the sovereign Creator of the universe wants to partner with us, but He does want this, and on many different levels.

One way to illustrate this is to imagine a farmer growing corn. The farmer does all he can to make the conditions ideal for corn to grow. He fertilizes the ground, prepares it for planting, sows the seed, waters the ground, pulls the weeds, and at just the right time, he harvests the crop. The farmer does his work, but he doesn't make the corn to grow. That's a miracle God Himself has built into each individual seed. All the farmer can do is enter into a partnership with God by creating the best conditions possible for the miracle of growth to occur. God does His part and when man does his part, the optimum results are achieved.

God's principle of partnership is only a general principle of His dealings with man. He's under no obligation to work with man in this way, and His ultimate purpose will not be frustrated by any failure of man to work with Him. It's God's right to act in a completely sovereign manner, without any cooperation with the efforts of man, and He does work this way more often than we suppose. However, as a general principle, it can be said that God works in partnership with man.

Paul understood this principle well. He told the Corinthians, *"We are God's fellow workers* [co-workers]" (1 Cor. 3:9). This principle of partnership helps us understand what he meant when he wrote about the possibility of God's grace being given in vain. If we neglect our part, then His grace doesn't accomplish what He has purposed, and it could be said that it was given in vain. But Paul determined that he wouldn't allow this to happen. He decided he would *labor abundantly* (1 Cor. 15:10) in cooperation with God's grace so that the best result would come to pass.

Many things keep us from working hard like Paul, and these things prevent us from seeing the greatest results from working with God. One obstacle is unbelief. We may choose to never appropriate the grace of God for daily living by faith, and refuse to live in the freedom and victory that such grace brings. We may slack off in our hard work because we're preoccupied with our own goals and projects, showing little interest for God's agenda. We must truly believe that furthering the Kingdom of God is more important than our own comfort and advancement if we are to work with the grace of God. Laziness may also keep us from the hard work that ensures the grace of God isn't given in vain. Such laziness can't be dealt with tenderly. God's call to the lazy Christian is to rise up from sleep and get busy working in partnership with Him (Eph. 5:14).

A preoccupation with hurt feelings or failure to truly forgive others may also prevent Christians from working together with God. When past hurt or sin against us influences our thinking and personality, it can take away the desire to look beyond our own problems and work in partnership with God to accomplish what is important to His kingdom. God's desire is that we leave all hurt, pain, and bitterness toward others at the cross and deal with these matters in a biblical manner. He wants us to *"forget those things which are behind... reaching forward to those things which are ahead"* (Phil. 3:13). With the help of God's grace, these things cannot hinder or keep us from laboring abundantly.

All of Grace

Those who are prone to the sin of pride know the great danger of working in partnership with God. It's easy to emphasize what we think we've done or to take all the credit for the glorious things God does when believers work together with Him. We can be like a flea that rides on the back of a lion and takes great pride that everyone's frightened. But Paul avoids this danger by understanding an important principle about our partnership with God. He realizes that even the effort he makes toward growth in righteousness is a result of God's grace. His hard work isn't a product of his own efforts, but the result of God's grace producing fruit in him. Paul writes, *"I labored more abundantly than they all, yet not I, but the grace of God which was with me"* (1 Cor. 15:10). Paul doesn't brag about his work or take credit for what he's done in partnership with God, for he realizes that it's only because of the work of grace that he was willing and able to do the work.

We can't boast about what we do in partnership with God either, because He supplies the grace that enables us to fulfill our partnership. Everything He expects from us in the Christian life, He provides the way to fulfill that expectation by His grace. And what does God expect from us apart from grace? One thing—total failure! God never intended that we'd be able to obey Him, do good works, and serve Him or His church apart from the transforming power of grace. He expects no performance from man until that one believes on Him and receives the grace that makes a godly life possible.

Now we can see that any failure to fulfill our duties when working in partnership with God is essentially a failure to receive and appropriate God's grace. Grace gives us the desire, the ability, and the resources to work hard, and when we fail to do that, it's because we haven't appropriated God's grace by faith for that specific purpose. Our growth, good works, and service in the Christian life are only works of grace, from beginning to end, and working with grace is vital for a fruitful life.

Paul's Plea

In this brief passage from 1 Corinthians, Paul enlightens the Christian's understanding and experience of grace. First, it's important to see that if people are going to change, it can only be through the power of grace. The law clearly tells us what we ought to be, but the law is powerless to help us change. Real change comes only through grace. Secondly, we understand that grace is a free gift, but it can be received in vain. If the reception of grace fails to bring about a spirit of obedience, good works, and a desire to serve both God and man, then grace has been received in vain and not properly received at all. To make sure that grace is not received in vain, God desires that we labor abundantly in partnership with Him to accomplish His work in our lives and in the world. Finally, Paul blocks our pride by pointing out that even our co-laboring with God is a result of His grace.

Paul's great desire for the Corinthians is that they would not be those who receive God's grace in vain. The Holy Spirit not only spoke to the Corinthians through Paul, but is also speaking to us. We need to understand and act on Paul's exhortation to every Christian: *"We then, as workers together with Him also plead with you not to receive the grace of God in vain"* (2 Cor. 6:1).

Chapter Ten

Falling from Grace

You have become estranged from Christ, you who attempt to be justified by law; you have fallen from grace. (Gal. 5:4)

The old legends about gods and goddesses of ancient Rome and Greece don't show them to be especially moral or righteous. Zeus, Apollo, Poseidon, and others were often known for their lying, cheating, sexual immorality, and cruelty. Therefore, one could be religious in ancient Rome and still be quite immoral, simply by following the pattern of their gods. This reminds us that religious people don't necessarily have or practice a high moral standard. We see a much higher level of conduct in the Old Testament, but even the lives of great patriarchs were filled with sin and moral failure. Abraham openly lied, Isaac cheated, Moses committed murder, and David committed both adultery and murder. We're amazed at what God did with such men and how He used them as an influence for godliness. But we also see that though these men had a high moral standard, they also had a hard time keeping that standard.

When compared to ancient religions, Christianity provides a sharp contrast. The gods of Olympus were admittedly immoral, and the heroes of Judaism couldn't live up to what they knew was right. In contrast, the essential figure of Christianity was a completely sinless man. Jesus Christ was absolutely pure and completely perfect

according to the most rigorous moral standards ever established—
God's. Jesus never sinned in word, action, or thought. He alone
could say, "*I always do those things that please Him* [God the Father]"
(John 8:29). No one but Jesus could face His bitter enemies and ask,
"*Which of you convicts Me of sin?*" (John 8:46). The fact that Jesus
Christ, our great example and model, was completely free from any
moral or spiritual imperfection presents a great challenge for those
who are called to be conformed into His image.

However, the perfection of Jesus can also be a stumbling block
to us, not because we fail to see His sinless nature, but because
His perfect life leads some to think that the goal of Christianity
is moral performance. We can think that *doing what Jesus did* is
more important than letting Him *live His life in us*. We know that
moral standards are important to Christianity, but are they the most
important thing in our faith? And what relationship does morality
have to salvation?

Morality and Salvation

At one time or another, most Christians think about the
relationship between morality and salvation. We usually think of
this relationship in terms of deciding what behaviors are appropriate
for those who claim to be followers of Jesus. We may look at those
who say they're Christians yet they do things that other believers
consider wrong and immoral. Some may smoke, drink, or dance;
others may use profanity or be sexually immoral. Inward sins are even
more dangerous, like greed, lust, and envy. When we see professing
Christians who compromise morally, it raises the question: Can a
failure in morality cause believers to lose their salvation?

Imagine someone who claims to be a Christian but is deeply
mired in sin. Choose the particular failure and the degree of
disobedience to form the hypothetical example in your mind; it
doesn't really matter what the type or degree of moral failure is. The
most important question is this: Can the moral failure cause this
person to lose their status as a Christian?

What Some Early Christians Thought

This question facing the Christian community isn't new. From its earliest days, the church has been confronted with the issue of how to deal with Christians who compromise morally.

Those who understand the heritage of the church are proud of its martyrs. We look back with admiration upon those brave believers who suffered or even died for their faith. Yet we must admit that there have been many Christians through the centuries who didn't stand strong in the face of persecution. The church has had its martyrs and its confessors, but it's also had cowards.

We know what to do with our martyrs—we admire them and honor the memory of their courage. But what about the cowards of the church? What do we do with those lapsed brothers who took the easy way out?

If this doesn't seem like an important problem to you, it's probably because you've never lived through a time of severe persecution. But in other times, this was a very important question for the church.

In the middle of the third century, Christians suffered severe persecution under the Roman emperor, Decian. Many found it easy to compromise in order to save their own lives. But when the season of persecution ended, they wanted back into the church fellowship, just as before.

Some groups said to these lapsed believers, "Come back freely. Just say you're sorry and all will be restored." These churches became notorious for a light view of sin among Christians because of the easy and painless path of restoration they offered.

Other Christians objected to such this casual view of sin. They went to the opposite extreme and said there was no way a lapsed Christian could ever be readmitted to salvation and the church.

These Christians earnestly believed that only one valid repentance was allowed after baptism. In other words, a newly baptized Christian could sin only once in a significant way and still be forgiven. After one sin, they believed that God no longer accepted the one who sinned. This was particularly true regarding the seven deadly sins of Idolatry, blasphemy, murder, adultery, fornication, false witness, and fraud. If Christians were guilty of any of these things twice after baptism, there could never be any hope for their salvation. This certainly was not the universal opinion of the church in that day, yet it was the firm belief of some.

A few of these groups during that period believed this so strongly that they broke away from the established church (in part or entirely) to protest its supposed softness in dealing with sinning believers. Groups such as the Montanists, the Novatians and the Donatists all thought that most other Christians were too lenient in receiving believers who had sinned, and they disassociated themselves because they believed in a higher standard.[67]

Today, most of us recognize that the groups who broke away were wrong. We understand that the blood of Jesus Christ is able to wash away the stain of any sin, if the sinner genuinely confesses and repents of it. Most would agree with the middle road of discipline, which the majority of Christians used to deal with such lapsed brothers: They allowed restoration, but required some kind of public confession and repentance that was clearly demonstrated. At the same time, we're justifiably offended by anyone who takes the title of "Christian" lightly, without realizing that the moral standard God calls us to is high, pure, and holy. But how can we walk in a balanced way between any two extremes? How can we understand the proper way to deal with moral failure in the church?

A Biblical Example

The best way is to see how the apostles dealt with sin in the church of their day. One of the most straightforward examples of this is in 1 Corinthians 5:1-5:

> *It is actually reported that there is sexual immorality among you, and such sexual immorality as is not even named among the Gentiles—that a man has his father's wife! And you are puffed up, and have not rather mourned, that he who has done this deed might be taken away from among you. For I indeed, as absent*

> *in body but present in spirit, have already judged, as*
> *though I were present, concerning him who has done*
> *this deed. In the name of the Lord Jesus Christ, when*
> *you are gathered together, along with my spirit, with*
> *the power of our Lord Jesus Christ, deliver such a one*
> *to Satan for the destruction of the flesh, that his spirit*
> *may be saved in the day of the Lord Jesus.*

This is a plain example of severe moral failure in the early church. Here we have a case of incest in the Corinthian assembly, a church member having sexual relations with his stepmother. Paul knew, and so did anyone else with an ounce of discernment, that such conduct was out of line with the behavior God expects of Christians. Therefore, Paul demanded a disciplinary excommunication of the man who was in sin. Paul expected that the Corinthians would no longer be proud of their supposed patience and forbearance with this man, but that they would immediately take action to separate him from the congregation.

Once the offender was outside the spiritual protection of the community of God's people, he was then on his own in the world, thought to be Satan's realm. In this way, he would be delivered over to Satan. But notice why Paul said this should be done. In His thinking, this wasn't to be done with the thought that it brings damnation upon the man; rather, it was to work toward his ultimate salvation.

Paul's words to the Thessalonians help us understand more about this strategy in dealing with those in the church who are caught in sin:

> *And if anyone does not obey our word in this epistle,*
> *note that person and do not keep company with him,*
> *that he may be ashamed. Yet do not count him as an*
> *enemy, but admonish him as a brother.* (2 Thess.
> 3:14-15)

We see that in both cases, Paul was serious about dealing with the sin of these people in the church. At the same time, this severe discipline was to be practiced in light of the fact that those in the wrong were still regarded as the family of God (*"admonish him as a brother"*) and eligible for eternal life (*"that his spirit may be saved in the day of the Lord Jesus"*). The point is this: Paul thought that in these specific cases, the guilty party must be dealt with according to the strict moral standard of the Christian faith, yet he didn't think their moral failure meant an immediate loss of salvation.

Paul gives another example of serious sin in the apostolic church:

> *Therefore, whoever eats this bread or drinks this cup of the Lord in an unworthy manner will be guilty of the body and blood of the Lord. But let a man examine himself, and so let him eat of the bread and drink of the cup. For he who eats and drinks in an unworthy manner eats and drinks judgment to himself, not discerning the Lord's body. For this reason many are weak and sick among you, and many sleep. For if we would judge ourselves, we would not be judged. But when we are judged, we are chastened by the Lord, that we may not be condemned with the world.* (1 Cor. 11:27-32)

In this passage, Paul addresses a serious problem in the Corinthian church. It seems that when they would meet together to take the Lord's Supper and remember His sacrifice, they'd disgrace the memory by their bad conduct. They would celebrate the Lord's Supper during a church-wide love feast (or potluck dinner), where everyone shared a common meal, and then take Communion together. But there wasn't a proper attitude of love and sharing among believers at these dinners, and some would become glutted and others would go home hungry. Paul said this kind of selfishness disgraced the spirit of the Lord's Supper. It was so serious that in the process of correcting the problem, God took some of them home to heaven. That is, some of the Corinthians were sick or even dead (*"and many sleep"*) because God determined that those believers had outlived their purpose on earth. This was a serious breaking of God's moral standards.

Yet notice again that even in the case of those who physically died because of their sin, God did not do this to condemn the guilty but to save them. The purpose of His severe judgment was to ensure that those in serious error might *not be condemned with the world.* So we see that even in this case of moral failure in the church, Paul didn't assume that the guilty party had lost their salvation. Instead, he acknowledged that the hand of God worked to help ensure it.

Receiving Grace

No one can read the New Testament without being impressed with the moral standards of Christianity. Yet the essence of Christianity is not the pursuit or attainment of a moral standard. As Paul said, "*For the kingdom of God is not eating and drinking, but righteousness and peace and joy in the Holy Spirit.*" (Rom. 14:17). The essence of Christianity is a living relationship with God through Jesus Christ on the principle of grace.

Seeing this helps us understand what it means to endure to the end in the Christian life. Both Calvinists and Arminians agree that true conversion is proved by perseverance. We remember Jesus' parable of the sower (Matt. 13:1-9, 18-23), where the truly fruitful seeds were those that endured. Some grew up quickly yet later withered away or were choked out by weeds. In this parable, Jesus illustrated that true Christianity is proven by perseverance.

However, we often misunderstand the central issue in perseverance—that *we are to persevere in grace.* We may easily fall into the error of considering perseverance only in terms of continuing in *works* and *moral behavior.* That is important, but we must first take care that we *continue in grace.*

The New Testament speaks strongly about this matter of continuing in grace. Remember that from God's end, grace can never fail. He never revokes His grace nor does He place a precondition of worth or merit on those who receive it by faith. Yet the New Testament indicates that a failure to *receive* grace can occur on the side of man. As Paul wrote in Galatians 1:6-7:

> *I marvel that you are turning away so soon from Him*
> *who called you in the grace of Christ, to a different*

gospel, which is not another; but there are some who trouble you and want to pervert the gospel of Christ.

Paul has in mind a real danger of turning away from the gospel of grace, which brings salvation. Later he wrote to the Galatians:

Stand fast therefore in the liberty by which Christ has made us free, and do not be entangled again with the yoke of bondage.... You have become estranged from Christ, you who attempt to be justified by law; you have fallen from grace. (Gal. 5:1, 4)

Paul was quite concerned that some in the Galatian church were in that danger of falling from grace. But what does it mean to fall from grace?

Considering what the entire New Testament says about grace, we can say that falling from grace does *not* mean that if a Christian happens to sin, he instantly falls from grace and is in danger of losing his salvation. The promises of Scripture are clear: if there is repentance, then sin causes us to fall *into* grace (if we receive it) because grace is for sinners! The acceptance and approval of grace isn't reserved for the few who can live up to a high and lofty standard. It's given freely without view of merit or demerit in the recipient, but with full view of the completed work of Jesus on Calvary.

Falling from grace is to let go of grace as the principle by which we connect to God, and to choose another principle instead. If we deny our right to relate to God on the principle of grace, we'll take up the principle of legalism to make that connection. In legalism, our relationship with God depends on our works instead of God's work. Legalism may promote itself under the guise of a genuine concern for holding up God's moral standard, but at its root, it communicates that Jesus' work isn't enough. The legalist believes that the work of Jesus is only of value if it's coupled with the works of the believer. Many who embrace legalism don't think of it by that name; they simply think it's an approach to God that makes sense. It may make sense to the flesh or to the natural man, but it makes no sense to the believer walking in the Spirit, who gladly embraces grace.

To fall from grace is to agree with any system in which the saving work of Jesus is substituted, in part or wholly, with the work of man. However, understand that no one falls from grace overnight. To truly reject grace as our principle of dealing with God requires a determined rejection of God's plan and revelation, and this can only happen over an extended period of time.

This danger of falling from grace helps explain the many New Testament exhortations to continue in grace:

> *Paul and Barnabas, speaking to them, persuaded them to continue in the grace of God.* (Acts 13:43)

> *They had been commended to the grace of God.* (Acts 14:26)

> *Paul chose Silas and departed, being commended to the grace of God.* (Acts 15:40)

> *And now, brethren, I commend you to God and the word of His grace, which is able to build you up and give you an inheritance among all those who are sanctified.* (Acts 20:32)

> *You therefore, my son, be strong in the grace that is in Christ Jesus.* (2 Tim. 2:1)

> *Pursue peace with all people, and holiness, without which no one will see the Lord; looking carefully lest anyone fall short of the grace of God.* (Heb. 12:14-15)

> *But grow in the grace and knowledge of our Lord and Savior Jesus Christ.* (2 Peter 3:18)

The theme is constantly emphasized: continue in grace, be entrusted (commended) to grace, be strong in grace, don't fall short of grace, and grow in grace. No wonder Paul was so concerned for those who were in danger of falling from grace!

The Big Debate

Does this mean that if a person has fallen from grace, they have lost their salvation? This is where we come back to that great debate between Calvinists and Arminians. One side says, "Once saved, always saved," and the other side says, "It's possible to lose your salvation." Some think Paul's warnings are certain proof that one can fall from grace and forfeit their salvation. Others think Paul simply used a dramatic warning and that it's impossible for anyone who has truly received saving grace to fall from it. Still others believe that the one who falls from grace simply loses blessings in this life, but not in eternal life.

Whatever your perspective is on the security of the believer's salvation, we can all unite in believing that continuing in grace is essential to enduring to the end in the Christian life. This endurance in grace is not a side issue to be dealt with after we make sure we're fulfilling a moral standard; it's absolutely central to following after Jesus. We understand that it's not enough to continue in good works or morality; we must never fall short of grace.

How Do You Know?

How can we tell if we're turning away from grace? This is one of those areas in the Christian life where what matters is the attitude of our heart. Falling from grace happens in the heart first, and we can't tell with certainty when it happens in another person. However, we can look for signs in ourselves that may indicate we're failing to continue in grace.

One frequent characteristic in those who turn away from grace is *pride*. Grace and pride are mutual enemies. When we fall from grace into an attitude of legalism, we soon begin to think we *earn* the blessings God gives. Under legalism, the major themes are earning and deserving instead of believing and receiving. This often nurtures a holy pride that takes a smug satisfaction in how right we live for God. The legalist is likely to take credit for any perceived spiritual accomplishments, while the believer continuing in grace is happy to give God all the glory.

Another characteristic of those who are unstable in grace is *insecurity* because when we relate to God in a legalistic way, we only sense His approval or acceptance when our performance measures up. Spurgeon considered the keeping power of God's grace in a sermon:

> "By the grace of God" we not only are what we are, but we also remain what we are. We should long ago have ruined ourselves, and damned ourselves, if Christ had not kept us by His Almighty grace.[68]

Under grace, our relationship with God is based on who He is and what He did for us. Under legalism, our relationship with God is based on who we are and what we do for Him.

Those who are in danger of falling from grace often display an *attitude of self-reliance*. Legalists think that the resources for holiness are within themselves and that all they must do is look within and try harder. This attitude influences the legalist's relationship with others, because he's not convinced of his need to rely on support and care from other Christians. Sadly, with such an emphasis on self-reliance, the one who drifts from grace is often defeated and discouraged on the inside, even if they look happy and victorious on the outside.

Finally, the one who doesn't properly relate to grace will often display a general coldness in their heart and life, because they don't connect to God in the way He has appointed. True joy of fellowship and communion with God can only come when we're obedient to God's plan and recognize the sovereignty of His system of grace.

There's one additional characteristic of the one who is falling from grace, but it must be seen in context. Most people think of moral failure as the main sign of turning away from grace, but obvious open moral failure may or may not be present in the one who turns away from grace. Remember that the legalists of Galatians 5:4 were very moral, at least by outward appearances, yet Paul warned about their falling from grace. When someone who claims to be a Christian doesn't meet the moral standard they are called to, it may indicate that they're turning away from grace, but that's not always the case. The essential point is that moral failure is a *symptom* in the one who turns away from grace; the turning away is the *root*. In guiding such a one back to Jesus, it's important to address the cause as well as the symptom. Many people simply address the symptoms, or the moral failure. They fail to speak to the need of the falling one to *embrace God's grace* as the ruling principle of their relationship to God and their entire life.

Continuing in Grace

It's also important to recognize the marks of the one who continues in grace. What does their life look like?

First, they show a genuine humility because they recognize that God did the work. Under grace, we realize that we don't get the credit, and our life is marked by a wonderful peace, for we know God is faithful even if we stumble. Our own salvation is based on what God did for us and in us, not on what we've done ourselves. Those who continue in grace show that they rely on God rather than themselves, and they openly confess their need to hear from Him. They also have a distinct boldness in life and ministry, understanding that God accepts them because of who He is and not because of who they are. They know that it is enough if God accepts and approves of them. They recognize that their salvation is not in danger if they happen to fail, so they're free to live boldly for Jesus. Most notably, and contrary to what the legalist thinks, as we continue in grace, we have the power to live in true victory and fruitfulness.

In light of Paul's truth, we see that many Christians focus on the wrong thing when they seek assurance of their salvation. True assurance cannot be measured by moral performance (though it's important and can't be ignored). The better measure is whether or not we're continuing in grace. If we focus only on moral performance, we run the risk of having a legalistic spirit that looks good outwardly but actually rejects God's truth and departs from His plan of grace. True assurance of salvation comes from diligently continuing in God's plan of grace, and recognizing that as we do, we'll have the proper tools necessary to fulfill the high moral standards of Christianity.

Chapter Eleven

Grace to Help

Let us therefore come boldly to the throne of grace, that
we may obtain mercy and find grace to help in time of
need. (Heb. 4:16)

In Revelation chapters 4 and 5, the apostle John has an amazing experience, being carried to heaven in some manner and seeing the throne of God. If you were to read these chapters and underline the word *throne* each time it's used, you'd see that John almost seems obsessed with the throne of God and the One who sits upon it. Everything in heaven is described in relation to the throne of God. One day, each Christian will see that throne, and there's no way to accurately describe the experience this side of eternity.

We might get the smallest idea of what it would be like by comparing it to the modern experience of meeting a king or queen or a famous celebrity. Imagine how anxious you'd feel, walking down a stately palace corridor and being ushered into the presence of the Queen of England. Most of us would be so nervous that it would be hard to enjoy the experience. Yet the nervousness—the sense of awe or dread—would be nothing compared to what it will be like to see our Great King on His heavenly throne. Any earthly comparison can't begin to illustrate what it will be like.

The closest we can come to understanding God's great throne is to carefully and prayerfully study what the Bible says about it. This is a subject mentioned many times in the Old Testament.

- *Righteousness and justice are the foundation of Your throne.* (Ps. 89:14)
- *God sits on His holy throne.* (Ps. 47:8)
- *Do not disgrace the throne of Your glory.* (Jer. 14:21)

From these verses, we may picture a sparkling white throne, full of glory, but not necessarily a place where we're welcomed. Several times Jesus' disciples fell at His feet when He displayed a small glimpse of His glory. How could we ever stand before the enthroned King of Heaven, sitting upon his just, holy, and glorious throne? It's almost as if the white-hot radiation of His holiness and glory would destroy anyone who came into His presence.

We should be thankful that the letter to the Hebrew Christians tells us more about the throne of God, and that it invites us—even *commands* us—to come to His throne. It's a throne of holy judgment, but it's also a throne of grace. The Old Testament portrays God's throne in pictures that might make us want to stay away. In fact, the ancient rabbis of Judaism taught that God had *two* thrones— one of mercy and one of judgment. They said this because they knew God was both merciful and just, but they couldn't understand how these two aspects could be combined into one. If they couldn't be reconciled, then perhaps God had two thrones to display the two aspects of His character. Upon one throne He would show His judgment, and upon the other He would show His mercy.

Happily, from our perspective on this side of the cross, we see mercy and judgment reconciled into one *throne of grace*. God's throne doesn't change into a throne of grace, but since the work of Jesus on the cross, it can now be revealed as a throne of grace and remain consistent with God's justice, judgment, holiness, and glory. This is a powerful lesson, showing us that grace isn't a matter of God simply overlooking our sin and deciding to forget about punishing it. Instead, grace is God acting righteously in view of the cross. Alexander Maclaren spoke eloquently about the significance of the throne of grace:

Whatever else there may be in the divine nature, the ruling sovereign element in Deity is unmerited love and mercy and kindly regard to us poor, ignorant, sinful creatures, which keeps pouring itself out over all the world. God is King, and the kingly thing in God is infinite grace.[69]

Therefore, when we come to this throne, we come to offer tribute to our King, but we also come to receive His great kingly gift of *"grace to help in time of need"* (Heb. 4:16).

Help!

The writer to the Hebrews tells us that we find *help* at the throne of grace, and we need the help of God. One of the saddest words in the English language is *helpless*, which describes one who is without help or beyond help. It's sad to be helpless, yet it's glorious to have free access to a throne of grace, where *grace to help* is freely given. When we come to understand our need for this help—that we're all as helpless as a turtle on its back—we come to the place where we can receive something from the throne of grace. We may come to this place because of distressing circumstances or because of the inward work of the Holy Spirit that persuades us of our need for God. In some way or another, God convinces us of our need so we can respond by seeking the help of grace.

It's wonderful that we find *help* at God's throne in our *time of need*. We don't find mere advice or sympathy—or worse yet—a committee; we find divine help in our time of need. God knows exactly how to best help those who have needs, and He loves to work through grace to meet those needs. Though many people think the Bible teaches that "God helps those who help themselves," you'll never find that statement in Scripture. This proverb was actually published in Benjamin Franklin's *Poor Richard's Almanac* of 1736, and from a Biblical perspective it should be changed to "God helps those who come by faith to the throne of grace to find grace to help in time of need."

When we need help, we need it at the right time. Ill-timed help is not helpful. The wagon train doesn't need the cavalry *before* the attack or *after* the attack, but at the right time. The writer to the Hebrews was careful to point out that we find help in time of need. This phrase *help in time of need* is literally translated "well-timed help" or "help at the right moment of time." Thankfully, we have a God who is more faithful than the cavalry, the Canadian Mountie, or the television hero who comes through at the right moment week after week. God not only knows what help we need, but He also knows exactly *when* we need it. Most of us have waited on God for something and been disappointed because we thought he delayed His help too long, only to see His perfect timing in retrospect.

We can be confident that the help God gives is more than enough to meet our needs. He gives according to His riches and glory, and His help is abundant and plentiful. He isn't stingy with assistance when we need it.

A story is told of a little boy who went down to the corner market to go shopping with his mother. The grocer wanted to be nice to the family, so he invited the boy to take a handful of cherries. Yet the boy seemed hesitant.

"Don't you like cherries?" asked the grocer.

"Sure," answered the boy.

The grocer then grabbed a big handful of cherries and poured them into the boy's outstretched hands. Later, his mother asked why he hadn't taken the cherries when first invited.

He quickly replied, "Because his hands were bigger than mine!"

When we come to God for help, He measures that gift according to *His* glory and majesty. He gives according to who He is and not according to who we are. He is a great God, one who loves to give great gifts to those who ask and trust in Him.

Notice what helps us in our time of need: the grace of God. This grace God gives helps in specific ways. It isn't just a mystical Band-Aid that God gives us in our time of need. Although the fullness of the help of grace is beyond our ability to list or describe, the New

Testament tells several practical things that grace helps us do. But before listing them, let's recall again what grace is—the unmerited love and favor of God that He pours out on those who come to Him through faith in His Son.

How Grace Helps

One of the most important ways grace helps is that it helps us obey God. As we've seen previously, Paul said that one reason grace is received is so that we might obey.

> *We have received grace and apostleship for obedience to the faith.* (Rom. 1:5)

We *need* help to be obedient Christians. It's never easy to persevere in obedience, and those who battle hard in the struggle to obey recognize that they can use all the help they can get. Grace steps in and helps us obey in several ways. It helps us obey when it gets our eyes off ourselves and puts our vision back on Jesus. Under grace we realize that there's nothing in us that can earn God's favor, and we know all our hopes and expectations must rest in Jesus and not in ourselves. Grace also helps us obey because it changes our motivation for obedience. Under grace, we feel no need to earn God's favor and approval, so we obey out of gratitude instead of by trying to repay a debt.

Another way grace helps us obey is that it teaches us how to please God—and how to please Him for the right reasons:

> *For the grace of God that brings salvation has appeared to all men, teaching us that, denying ungodliness and worldly lusts, we should live soberly, righteously, and godly in the present age.* (Titus 2:11-12)

If we really want to please God with our obedience, we should register in His school of grace and allow grace to teach us about obeying Him. Notice that the same grace that brings salvation also instructs us in the way of godly living. We can't receive the salvation of grace apart from the teaching of grace, which instructs us in obedience.

Another way grace helps us is in our worship. Paul considered a heart full of grace as essential for worship that was pleasing to God: He said:

> *Let the word of Christ dwell in you richly in all wisdom, teaching and admonishing one another in psalms and hymns and spiritual songs, singing with grace in your hearts to the Lord.* (Col. 3:16)

Worship is a learned activity. Our worship of God is only as rich as our appreciation of who He is and what He's done for us. If we don't know about the nature and work of grace, we can't worship in full measure. An experiential knowledge of grace will radically affect our worship, giving us an awe-struck gratitude toward God. Believers who walk in grace worship freely because they're able to set their focus completely on Jesus and not on themselves.

One area that often needs the help grace brings is the way we talk. It's always easy to say things that tear others down instead of building them up. Sarcastic, critical, and disrespectful words seem to flow easily from our tongue. Yet the New Testament tells us that God has ordained grace to help us speak properly, in a way that brings glory to Him:

> *Let your speech always be with grace, seasoned with salt, that you may know how you ought to answer each one.* (Col. 4:6)

When we've truly received grace, we can't help being givers of God's unmerited love and favor to others. We can be channels of God's unmerited favor by what we say. Will we speak words that express our unconditional love and acceptance of others, or will we say (or imply) that our love depends on their performance? When our words are seasoned with grace, we'll have the desire and ability to speak words that bring comfort, assurance, and encouragement. We'll build others up by what we say rather than tear them down.

Grace helps us say what we ought to in other situations as well. When we're placed in circumstances where we have the opportunity to defend our faith, grace can help us speak forth the way we should, assuring us of God's abiding approval. Therefore, we can speak boldly, without a heart that begs for man's approval. We can be free to tell the truth in love, because even if others reject us, we're confident of God's acceptance.

Grace also helps us to serve God in an acceptable manner, as we read in Hebrews 12:28:

> *Therefore, since we are receiving a kingdom which cannot be shaken, let us have grace, by which we may serve God acceptably with reverence and godly fear.*

One of the biggest ways grace helps us serve God is that it prompts us to serve Him with the proper motivation. Under grace, we recognize God's righteousness, and we serve Him out of gratitude instead of proudly congratulating ourselves on the good things we do for Him. Serving out of a desire to earn favor from the Lord is not acceptable service. It's also wrong to do things for God while thinking He will then be obligated to do something for us. This attitude offends God's truth and glory because if we think we can put Him in our debt by our service to Him, then our service is not acceptable in His sight.

Paul had the right perspective in his service for God. He knew that his ministry was an enabling of grace:

> *I became a minister according to the gift of the grace of God.... This grace was given, that I should preach among the Gentiles the unsearchable riches of Christ.* (Eph. 3:7-8)

In whatever way you serve among God's people (and everyone is called to serve in some way), make sure that your work is done under the motivation and enabling of grace. If it's not directed by grace, then your service may not be acceptable to God.

Grace also helps us become givers. It's easy for many Christians to let Jesus be Lord over everything *except* their finances. Surrendering our financial life to Jesus rarely comes easy, and we must be instructed and assisted by grace so we can learn to be cheerful givers:

> *So we urged Titus, that as he had begun, so he would also complete this grace in you as well. But you abound*

> *in everything—in faith, in speech, in knowledge, in*
> *all diligence, and in your love for us—see that you*
> *abound in this grace also.... And God is able to make*
> *all grace abound toward you, that you, always having*
> *all sufficiency in all things, have an abundance for*
> *every good work.* (2 Cor. 8:6-7, 9:8)

The grace Paul spoke of in this passage is the grace that leads us to be givers. Paul encouraged these Corinthian Christians to give generously for the benefit of the poor and starving Christians in Jerusalem. After all, they abounded in faith, speech, knowledge, diligence, and love; now it was time for them to also abound in their ability to give.

Grace teaches us to give with a right attitude. When Jesus spoke about the widow who gave her two mites, He showed that it isn't how much we give that impresses God, it's our attitude in giving that He's interested in. We can't give with the right heart if we don't realize that giving is to be a work of grace. This isn't only true in financial giving, but in all giving.

The sacrificial giving of Jesus—giving all He had and all He was—demonstrated His amazing grace to man. He was willing to give everything, and to give it freely for the benefit of all who might receive. When we receive this grace and understand it, we can't help but respond by becoming givers ourselves. The stingy person is afraid he might give too much, but the grace-filled person knows that because of grace, he will never out-give God. God's display of grace in Christ shows Him to be the supreme giver.

One of the most significant ways grace helps us is by building an established heart within us. The writer to the Hebrews points this out:

> *Do not be carried about with various and strange*
> *doctrines. For it is good that the heart be established by*
> *grace.* (Heb. 13:9)

Strange doctrines often sweep through the church, making it all the more important that our hearts be established by grace. Paul warned:

For the time will come when they will not endure sound doctrine, but according to their own desires, because they have itching ears, they will heap up for themselves teachers; and they will turn their ears away from the truth, and be turned aside to fables. (2 Tim. 4:3-4)

It certainly feels like that time is now, and with our extensive global communications, it's amazing how quickly deception can spread all over the world. Yet if we establish our hearts with grace, it has a way of making our ears less itchy and makes us less likely to turn aside to fables. Grace, when applied biblically in the life of the believer, has a remarkable ability to establish the heart of the one who receives it. Coming to God on the principle of grace (as opposed to law) gives us the peace and security of knowing that salvation and blessing are not earned, but freely given and received by genuine faith.

Walking in grace keeps us on the correct path doctrinally and keeps our hearts from going after "various and strange doctrines." An understanding of God's unmerited favor also helps us test strange doctrines, because false teachings often reject the biblical teaching of grace. For example, some false teachings promote the idea that salvation results from works *and* grace, and that we must work as hard as we can for our salvation, and then somehow grace will make up what's missing. This isn't true! Salvation is *all* of grace, and we're saved *for* good works, not *by* good works. Others preach a pseudo-grace that doesn't transform us unto obedience and doesn't teach godly living. Again, we know that whenever true grace reigns, righteousness will also reign. Some imply in their teaching that God gives to believers out of obligation, denying God's motive of giving because of unmerited favor in Jesus. Grace helps establish our hearts, because one way to test false doctrines is to examine their teachings concerning grace.

Rejecting This Help

Unfortunately, some people choose to reject the help God offers in His grace. Yet, rejecting this grace causes great danger. The New Testament shows many ways grace helps us in our time of need.

- Grace helps us to *obey* (Rom. 1:5).
- Grace helps us to *worship* (Col. 3:16).
- Grace helps us to *speak rightly* (Col. 4:6).
- Grace helps us to *serve God* (Heb. 12:28).
- Grace helps us to *give* (2 Cor. 8:6-7, 9:8).
- Grace helps us to become *established in the truth* (Heb. 13:9).

The defeated, dry Christian often refuses the help of grace and trusts in his own abilities to do what God wants to help him with. Sometimes this dependence on self brings temporary and outward success, but it's useless in the long course of the Christian life. Remember that to be disappointed in yourself is to have trusted in yourself, and to be helpless is to not come to the throne of grace to find help. Many people want to do all the right things with godly intentions, but their attempts are rooted in self. These individuals especially need to receive the instruction and help of grace.

Coming to His Throne

Some people don't like to think about appearing before God's throne. They live each day without really knowing if they' are completely accepted by Him or not. They would rather not think about the return of Jesus, because they aren't sure how they'll be received by Him. But the Word of God teaches that we *can* appear before a throne of grace, right now and on that day in the life to come. If we've received grace by faith in Jesus during this life, then we can also enjoy that grace in the life to come.

If we reject Jesus Christ and His plan of salvation by grace, we have to answer at the great white throne of judgment. The apostle John wrote:

> *Then I saw a great white throne and Him who sat on it, from whose face the earth and the heaven fled away. And there was found no place for them. And I saw the dead, small and great, standing before God, and books were opened. And another book was opened, which is*

the Book of Life. And the dead were judged according to their works, by the things which were written in the books. (Rev. 20:11-12)

We have the privilege now of choosing which throne we will come to. Actually, there is only one throne, but we choose to come to that throne either as rebels deserving judgment or as servants receiving grace. And *"how shall we escape if we neglect so great a salvation?"* (Heb. 2:3).

It's good to think ahead to the day when we'll actually stand before that awesome throne of God. When we think ahead to that day, we should be thankful that it's a throne of grace, of unmerited favor, that's received by genuine faith in Jesus Christ. We should also be challenged to know that if we hear Jesus say, "Well done, you good and faithful servant, enter into the joy of your Lord," it will be because we've been a servant by the power and work of grace. We rest in knowing that all which isn't of grace will be burned away, and those ashes count for nothing before His throne of grace. In seeking the help we need for living the Christian life, we should live by the motto, "All is of grace; and grace is for all."

Chapter Twelve

Grace and Pride

God resists the proud, but gives grace to the humble.
(1 Peter 5:5)

God resists the proud—it's a proven fact again and again through the pages of the Bible. When Israel demanded a king, God chose Saul, who was a very humble man. But Saul's heart was soon raised up in pride, and he rebelled against God and His word. It wasn't long until the Lord took the kingdom away from Saul and gave it to a humble shepherd named David.

God also humbled King Nebuchadnezzar of Babylon when the king grew proud. In the height of Nebuchadnezzar's regal glory and splendor, God struck him with madness until he came to renounce his pride and give glory to the God of heaven. In Jesus' ministry too, we see that He often confronted the pride of man. His strongest rebukes weren't directed toward adulterers or drunkards, but to the self-righteous and proud religious people of His day.

It's helpful to ask *why*. Why is pride such a big sin? Why is God opposed to pride and honored by man's humility? In his book *Mere Christianity*, C.S. Lewis, explains part of the answer:

> According to Christian teachers, the essential vice, the utmost evil, is Pride. Unchastity, anger, greed, drunkenness, and all that are mere fleabites in

comparison: it was through Pride that the devil became the devil: Pride leads to every other vice: it is the complete anti-God state of mind.[70]

Lewis then expounds on the dangerous nature of pride:

The other, and less bad, vices come from the devil working on us through our animal nature. But this does not come through our animal nature at all. It comes direct from Hell. It is purely spiritual: consequently it is far more subtle and deadly.[71]

Satan's grand strategy is to turn us into proud religionists with no true relationship to Jesus. He tries to work within us the attitude of the publican in Jesus' parable from Luke 18:9-14: "*God, I thank you that I am not like other men*," rather than the attitude of the tax collector: "*God, be merciful to me a sinner*." The devil prizes one proud saint more than a whole flock of miserable sinners. When he looks at a believer who is walking in pride, he can say, "Now there's someone like me! Aware of spiritual things, yet utterly infected with the cancer of pride."

Though Satan's great work is to turn us into proud religionists, God has a completely different purpose for us. Satan's infernal goal is to re-create us after his own hellish likeness, but God's great plan is to fully restore His image in us. And He has appointed a specific way to start and complete this work of restoration. *Grace* is the great weapon God uses to advance His plan; *pride* is the devil's main tool in his destructive work. An understanding of grace enables us to stand against the devil's subtle strategy of making us proud.

How We Get Grace

God's favor is valuable. The word Paul uses for *favor* in the ancient Greek language expresses how highly regarded this favor was in his day. In the time Paul wrote, the word *grace* (charis) was used to describe the imperial favor by which gifts were given to the cities and people of the Roman Empire.[72] If the attitude of the emperor toward you was charis, it meant you enjoyed a status and privilege that those outside the emperor's grace didn't know. To receive this grace meant that you (or your city) were held in special regard by the emperor of Rome. Yet the favor of God is much greater than the regard of any human emperor. To be a receiver of His grace means that you're important to Him; He considers you one of His special friends.

But how can we gain this status of favor in God's eyes? It may help to understand how we approach gaining the favor of others. Children who are hungry for acceptance learn early what must be done to gain a parent's approval; they understand what behaviors receive praise and what behaviors earn disapproval in school. We all learn that to gain the favor of a teacher, we must be good. We discover what a teacher requires for the grade we want, and we set out to meet those standards according to our teacher's requirements.

Later, we learn that to gain the favor of a politician, we must contribute a big check to his campaign fund. To gain the favor of someone who's popular, we must do things to make that person feel more popular. All these methods are generally successful in gaining the favor of others, but none of them work in obtaining favor from God. We can't gain God's grace by being good, nor can we contribute enough money to His work to earn His approval. It's true that we can gain the favor of others by praise and flattery, and though God is worthy of our honor and worship, even the sweetest praise can't give us the special status before God that grace can give. And so we ask, "How do we receive this grace?"

Theologians argue over the answer. The Roman Catholic Church teaches that grace is obtained through Catholicism—that their church is like a "bank" of grace. They believe that great saints through the centuries were so good that they received grace they didn't need, so they deposited their "extra" grace into the church. We can withdraw this grace by performing different sacraments. Thomas Torrance explains the Roman Catholic view on how grace is received:

> The Church as the body of Christ was looked on as
> the depository of pneumatic [spiritual] grace, which

might be dispensed in sacramentalist fashion after
the analogy of the mystery religions. The Church, in
other words, possessed the means of grace.[73]

This way of seeing the church as a bank of grace actually began
early in Christian theology. For example, Ignatius (who died
sometime between AD 98 and AD 117) thought that grace and its
distribution was especially located in the church's bishops. This was
later thought to mean that the priest or the bishop functioned as
something like a teller at the church's "bank of grace." Through the
sacraments he offered, the extra grace of the saints was made available
to the common man or woman. Thus, in the Roman Catholic view,
grace is obtained through the church by receiving the sacraments.

It's understandable why people started thinking this way. After
all, it some saints seemed to deserve and earn so much grace that
they couldn't possibly use it all, and others earned and deserved so
little. It was believed that the godly saints wouldn't mind sharing
their extra grace with those who needed it. Nevertheless, this view
on receiving grace contradicts the New Testament's teaching. The
Bible teaches that grace is received as a gift from Jesus to be directly
received by the believer without going through the church, the
priest, or the sacraments. For example, Paul told the Corinthians:

> I thank my God always concerning you for the grace of
> God which was given to you by Christ Jesus. (1 Cor.
> 1:4)

When we consider the earthly ministry of Jesus Christ, we see
that He was a constant giver of grace. Jesus was always bestowing His
favor and approval on those who came to Him by faith, quite apart
from their merits or their deserving anything. Christ continues this
work today, freely giving grace to those who believe. Paul repeats
this theme of receiving grace from Jesus often:

- *Through Him* [Jesus] *we have received grace.* (Rom.1:5)

- *Through whom* [Jesus] *also we have access by faith into this grace
  in which we stand.* (Rom. 5:2)

- *According to the riches of His grace which He* [Jesus] *made to abound toward us.* (Eph. 1:7-8)

Thomas Torrance states that the church began to go wrong in its doctrine of grace when it separated receiving grace from the person of Jesus, and that this error began to slip in early in the history of the church. People were so aware of the holiness and perfection of Jesus that they found it hard to believe they could come to Christ directly for this precious and unmerited favor.[74]

Because Jesus teaches us to come directly through Him to the Father (John 14:6), we must guard ourselves from thinking we need any other mediator to receive His acceptance and approval The New Testament never tells us that a believer must go through anyone but Jesus to receive His grace.

Who Wants Grace?

With this amazing direct access to God's favor available to everyone, we might wonder why people aren't willing to stand in line to receive God's grace. Think of what would happen if the following announcement was released from the White House by the President: "Everyone who comes to the White House next Wednesday at noon will be regarded as a special friend of the President of the United States." I suppose some people wouldn't care, but of course there would be a line beginning at 1600 Pennsylvania Avenue and stretching for miles. Many would want to take advantage of such an offer. Yet why don't people respond in the same way to God's offer?

The answer has to do with a special characteristic of the person who seeks and finds the grace of God. The Scriptures tell us that receiving grace depends on humility:

> *God resists the proud, but gives grace to the humble.*
> (1 Peter 5:5, James 4:6, each quoting the idea in
> Proverbs 3:34)

This straightforward statement about receiving God's grace is repeated three times in the Bible. The Holy Spirit repeats Himself for good reason. There's special truth here that God wanted to emphasize so He wrote it in triplicate! This is the essence of that truth: *The proud reject grace because grace refuses to consider any merit or worthiness that people think they have.* Remember that grace, by definition, is unmerited favor, given apart from any consideration of merit in the receiver. Proud people don't want anything to do with a system that doesn't take into account how marvelous they are; therefore, they reject grace and are resisted by God. Grace and pride are irreconcilable enemies, because pride demands to have its merits glorified, and grace refuses to consider those merits.

On the other hand, the humble realize their own unworthiness and their complete inability to attain worthiness, yet they find themselves blessed on another principle outside themselves. These are the ones who say, "God, be merciful to me a sinner," recognizing that He owes them nothing but judgment. When they come to God with this humility, they find His favor and approval waiting for them. All who will come to God must come with an honest recognition of their unworthiness.

It isn't that we *earn* grace by our humility; instead, the humble naturally receive God's grace, which is given freely in Jesus. Pride proves that we have a fundamental disagreement with God's plan of grace because grace isn't based on earning and deserving. When we are humble, it proves we're in agreement with that plan, recognizing both our unworthiness and God's greatness.

Holding Back Pride

We know that only those who set aside their pride will want to come to God by the way of grace. But it's also important to see that as we walk in grace, grace holds back the dangerous infection of pride in the life of the Christian.

An understanding of grace keeps us from being proud about our salvation. As Paul wrote:

> For by grace you have been saved through faith, and
> that not of yourselves; it is the gift of God, not of works,
> lest anyone should boast. (Eph. 2:8-9)

When we know that our salvation and position of favor with

God is according to grace and not works, how can we be proud? What do we have to boast about? It's all due to the grace and goodness of God. Therefore, to be proud is to be blind, for we have no standing in ourselves; all our boasting is in Jesus. God did it this way to promote humility in the human race, which finds it easy to glory in self.

God designed creation to build this humility into man's soul. This purpose was not lost upon the Psalmist:

> *When I consider Your heavens, the work of Your fingers, the moon and the stars, which You have ordained, what is man that You are mindful of him, and the son of man that You visit him?* (Ps. 8:3-4)

If God's creative work in nature was meant to teach us humility, how much more should we be humbled by the re-creative work that God does in the life of the believer? Everyone in Jesus is a new creature, and a true appreciation of this fact always produces a new creature who doesn't boast of his or her own merits and worth.

Believers who occasionally fall into pride and boastfulness must be a great source of amazement to the angels looking down from heaven. The angels must wonder, *What do they have to boast about? Can't they see it's all the work of God's grace?* And what about those who habitually exhibit pride and boastfulness? Living this way contradicts true belief in God. No one who genuinely receives and experiences the grace of God can possibly live a life characterized by habitual pride. Such a person must examine their own heart to see if they've been deceived by a false conversion. Charles Spurgeon put it this way:

> He who says to himself, "I am righteous; I can stand before God and deserve his love," is as surely lost as though he had fallen into gross sin. Take heed of the Pharisee that lurks within you.[75]

The principle of grace helps correct our pride regarding our own salvation, and it also helps us avoid other common pitfalls of pride in the Christian life. For example, many Christians become proud and boastful about their supposed maturity and spiritual accomplishments. They fail to recognize that spiritual growth is not earned; it's a gift of grace. As we abide in Jesus, we'll naturally grow and bear fruit for God. It isn't that we've earned spiritual growth by our discipline and diligence, but we've put ourselves in a position to receive it as a free gift from God.

Another way many Christians stumble into pride is in the area of ministry. It can be easy to get boastful and proud over the idea that God has chosen us to a particular ministry. Paul had the mindset that kept him from this danger. He repeatedly took the opportunity to say in his letters that he recognized his calling and ministry were not the result of his worthiness, but because of God's grace:

> *For we are God's fellow workers; you are God's field, you are God's building. According to the grace of God which was given to me, as a wise master builder I have laid the foundation, and another builds on it.* (1 Cor. 3:9-10)

> *But by the grace of God I am what I am, and His grace toward me was not in vain; but I labored more abundantly than they all, yet not I, but the grace of God which was with me.* (1 Cor. 15:10)

> *But when it pleased God, who separated me from my mother's womb and called me through His grace, to reveal His Son in me, that I might preach Him among the Gentiles.* (Gal. 1:15-16)

It's sad that ministers and other leaders in the church can be vain and proud, thinking their ministry is the most important and competing with others for the limelight. It's also tragic that many leaders enjoy the distinction between "clergy" and "laity," and some enter the ministry to bolster a low self-image. But Paul serves as an excellent example of someone who understood that his call and work were based on God's unmerited favor; there was nothing of his own deserving in it. Indeed, it's hard to imagine a more undeserving person for ministry than Saul of Tarsus, yet God called him. Because it's characteristic of God's grace to not wait for human performance, His grace can call such a one as Saul the persecutor and transform him into Paul the apostle. The great missionary and theologian of the apostolic church knew there was no place for pride or self-glorying in his ministry, and we should admit the same concerning any ministry God has called us to.

Another area where we're vulnerable to pride is in the supernatural gifts given by the Holy Spirit for service in the body of Christ. Paul was careful to tell us that these gifts are given on the basis of grace, not works:

> But to each one of us grace was given according to the measure of Christ's gift.... And He Himself gave some to be apostles, some prophets, some evangelists, and some pastors and teachers. (Eph. 4:7, 11)

> For I say, through the grace given to me, to everyone who is among you, not to think of himself more highly than he ought to think, but to think soberly, as God has dealt to each one a measure of faith.... Having then gifts differing according to the grace that is given to us, let us use them: if prophecy, let us prophesy in proportion to our faith; or ministry, let us use it in our ministering; he who teaches, in teaching; he who exhorts, in exhortation; he who gives, with liberality; he who leads, with diligence; he who shows mercy, with cheerfulness. (Rom.12:3, 6-8)

Whatever your view is on the gifts of the Holy Spirit and their place in the life of the church, you probably know some people who exercise such gifts in an attitude of superiority. Paul is careful to note that there's absolutely no basis for that attitude. Not only are the gifts given by grace, they're also expressions of grace. This is indicated by the specific words Paul uses to describe spiritual gifts in the original language of the New Testament. *Charis* (grace) is the root of *charisma* (spiritual gift). Paul is saying that these spiritual gifts are, in fact, *grace gifts*. At their very root, they are undeserved and unmerited. It seems that Paul invented this term to express the thought of a gift given on the basis of grace. When we understand that these gifts are given on such a basis, it serves as a guard against self-congratulation, self-importance, or an attitude of pride about any spiritual gift. After all, how can we be proud about something given completely apart from merit? Our pride over these grace gifts is a mystery.

Grace and Glory

If understanding grace effectively takes the focus off our own merits and worthiness, it is also equally effective in putting the focus on God's majestic character and holiness. Therefore, God made a way for us to become channels of His grace to others. We can impart grace to others by what we say:

> Let no corrupt word proceed out of your mouth, but what is good for necessary edification, that it may impart grace to the hearers. (Eph. 4:29)

God wants us to receive His grace and then imitate Him by loving others and encouraging them, whether they deserve it or not. We have the opportunity to display God's favor to others by showing them a love and acceptance that isn't based on their merits or performance. By our words, we have special opportunity to do this because what we say will either express a gracious attitude or one that bases acceptance on performance. One way God communicates His grace is by the grace-filled words He spoke to us. We give grace to others in the same way, by assuring them of our love and favor, even when they feel undeserving.

Peter expresses this idea about grace in his first letter:

> As each one has received a gift, minister it to one another, as good stewards of the manifold grace of God. (1 Peter 4:10)

Notably, the word Peter uses for *gift* here is *charisma*, the same word Paul uses for "spiritual gifts" or "grace gifts." Peter said that we're to act as good stewards of God's grace. We often hear about being good managers of our money, but we don't often hear that we should be good managers of the grace God gives us. The Lord entrusts us with grace so we might become distributors of it to others in need. Of course, no one can actually distribute the grace of God that's necessary for salvation, but we can be examples of the giving and loving character of grace. This kind of life will spark an interest and prepare the hearts of those who have yet to come to God through Jesus to receive His favor and approval by faith. As faithful stewards of God's unmerited favor, we can reach out to those who won't come to His grace and give them a glimpse of it through our gracious living. After they see grace displayed in us, we can then introduce them to God and His saving grace.

In carrying out our duty to be "good stewards of the manifold grace of God," humility is crucial. If we regard this responsibility as a reward for faithful service, we'll minister to others with a condescending mentality that conveys, *I think I'm better than you.* Without letting go of pride, we'll draw attention to the *steward* rather than *the manifold grace of God.*

This spreading of grace through those who receive it brings thanks and glory to God. Paul, always speaking of grace, said:

> For all things are for your sakes, that grace, having spread through the many, may cause thanksgiving to abound to the glory of God. (2 Cor. 4:15)

When people see the outworking of grace in our lives and hear our testimony of the changes it brings, many will give thanks and glorify God as the great giver of grace. This is the goal of walking in grace: to bring glory to God in gratitude for what He's done for us. The desire to see Him glorified becomes our motivation for being good stewards of His grace. And if the Master is glorified, the servant is satisfied.

Two Ways

In God's plan, we can receive His grace directly from Jesus, but only those who come in humility will want or find grace. This is because pride—the opposite of humility—is an enemy of grace. Grace sees merit only in Jesus, and pride demands recognition of its own merit. We also understand that our salvation, our ministry, and our spiritual gifts are all granted on the basis of grace; therefore, we can take no credit for any of them. In the plan of God's grace, we also have the opportunity to bring glory to Him by being channels, or stewards, of that grace. Giving grace to others imitates the way He gives it to us.

All we have in Jesus, we have by grace. We add to that a genuine desire to be a channel of God's grace to others. Only with this mindset can we stay on guard against the infection of pride. In a sense, there are two armies at war and each one seeks recruits. To enlist in the army of hell, we learn the ways of pride and self-glorying. To enlist in heaven's army, we're required to learn the ways of grace and humility. We must take great care to make sure we're on the right side in the continuing war between grace and pride.

Chapter Thirteen

Eternal Grace

In my hometown of Santa Barbara, one of my favorite places is the hills along its northern boundary. When I drive up into those hills, I can look out on the breathtaking view of the entire city. From this vantage point, I take in the whole coastline, and on a clear day the view stretches out over the blue Pacific with the Channel Islands off in the distance. When out-of-town guests come to visit, I enjoy taking them up in the hills so they can see this beautiful perspective too. This view also helps them understand how the city is put together and keeps them from getting lost.

Once we have an overview of something, we can more easily understand how the specifics fit together. This is especially true when considering God's plan for the human race.

We gain a lot from a careful study of God's plan of the ages for creation and the human race. Most of us find it easy to miss the broad themes of the Bible, and we think of Scripture as a collection of individual verses instead of a story from beginning to end. It's one thing to be aware of God's love in our own experience, but our experiences are limited. To see how God has displayed His love for us through all of eternity gives a fresh perspective on a familiar truth. There's similar blessing in charting the course of any aspect of God's character or plan, beginning in eternity past and following all the way to the age to come. Although there's great benefit in conducting a detailed study of each aspect of God's plan of the ages, our focus is on what the Bible says about the place of God's grace in this eternal plan.

Grace in Eternity Past

> *Who has saved and called us with a holy calling, not according to our works, but according to His own purpose and grace which was given to us in Christ Jesus before time began.* (2 Tim. 1:9)

It stretches our minds to imagine it, but Paul tells us here that God gave His grace to His people *before time began.* There's a lot we don't know about this. We don't know exactly how God's work of grace connects with our free choice—before time began. We don't know how God could give grace unto salvation to His saints when they existed only in His knowledge of the future. And we also don't know how God could give grace to people who aren't even created yet.

A partial explanation of this great mystery is that this grace was given to us *"in Christ before time began."* We can more readily understand that the Father and the Son had a mutual relationship of grace in eternity past. Paul tells us that because we're identified with Christ, we're made heirs to that same eternal relationship of grace. And because we *"are all sons of God through faith in Christ Jesus"* (Gal. 3:26), we share in the benefits of Christ's sonship. One of those benefits is the heritage of an eternal grace. In some way beyond our full comprehension, God had an eternal plan for us.

To realize that the plan of grace for us began in eternity past is a striking revelation. God's decision to deal with man on the basis of grace was not a new or late decision. Our Creator isn't an inefficient planner who tried His best with one method, found it didn't work, and then went on to another method. God didn't suddenly decide to abandon an ineffective system of law in dealing with man; law was a necessary preparation for the system of grace. Though the ways of law and grace are irreconcilable methods of relating to God, the law beautifully prepares the mind, heart, and soul of man for God's embrace of unmerited favor.

Grace isn't a new thing in God's plan, and this is demonstrated by His promise of a Messiah. At the first appearing of man's need, God gave the solemn promise of a coming Savior from sin and demonic deception. God assured both man and Satan that One would come from the seed of the woman who would crush the head of Satan and end his ability to hold mankind in chains. Yes, the Messiah Himself would be bruised in the course of the battle, but He would also deliver a death-wound to the devil and all his kind. Grace was implicit in such an ancient promise of a Messiah-Redeemer. The promise was motivated by the gracious love of God. Did mankind deserve such a redeemer or earn such a promise? When were we ever so good or kind or loving so as to be worthy of such assurance? We never merited such a plan of redemption, but the giving of the promise of the Messiah was an ancient evidence of God's plan of grace.

When we consider the history of grace, we also think of how God displayed His gracious nature throughout His dealings with Israel and the patriarchs in the Old Testament. Think about Jacob—a sneaking, devious cheater—who lied to his father and stole his brother's birthright. Did he deserve that birthright? Did he earn the right to God's amazing protection and blessing upon his family and finances? Of course, he didn't earn those blessings, but God gave them out of the riches of His grace.

Consider Moses, who was a murderer and a fugitive. He did nothing to make God say, "Well, Moses has earned the right to lead his people and experience the most intimate communion with Me that any man has ever had." God granted these privileges and blessings to Moses on the basis of grace, not works or merit. God's working in the lives of men like Jacob and Moses shows that He deals with men and women by a system of grace, apart from what they deserve. Though grace came in fullness through Jesus Christ, the God of all grace had to reveal this aspect of His character in His dealings with mankind before the coming of Jesus.

Grace in the Here and Now

The good news for us is that even though God's grace is ancient and reaches back into eternity past, it's also modern and ready to meet us where we are today. As believers, our present standing before God is characterized by grace:

> *I have written to you briefly, exhorting and testifying*
> *that this is the true grace of God in which you stand.*
> (1 Peter 5:12)

We're secure in a position of favor and blessing to be received by faith, not earned by good deeds. As we enjoy this favor, we also receive the desire and ability to serve God rightly. Having received so much, we're then to labor and honor God by our obedience, working for His kingdom and doing it all out of gratitude for His blessings. Grace also enables us to stand and persevere in spiritual battle. We know that God is for us, not against us.

Peter tells us something else that's important about grace in the here and now:

> *But grow in the grace and knowledge of our Lord and*
> *Savior Jesus Christ.* (2 Peter 3:18)

Peter wants Christians to remember that grace should remain an essential part of our growth and maturity. We grow *in* grace, not *beyond* it. Grace is to remain our life principle of connecting to God. Charles Spurgeon, the great preacher of Victorian England, spoke powerfully to this point:

> But you will remark that our text does not say
> anything about grace growing; it does not say that
> grace grows. It tells us to "grow in grace." There is
> a vast difference between grace growing and our
> growing in grace. God's grace never increases; it is
> always infinite, so it cannot be more; it is always
> everlasting; it is always bottomless; it is always
> shoreless. It cannot be more; and, in the nature of
> God, it could not be less. The text tells us to "grow
> in grace." We are in the sea of God's grace; we cannot
> be in a deeper sea, but let us grow now we are in it.[76]

Grace in Eternity Future

The apostle Peter saw that grace was for us today, in the here and now, but he also knew that the work of grace wouldn't be over when we graduate from this earthly existence; grace would be given to us at the return of Jesus Christ:

> *Therefore gird up the loins of your mind, be sober, and*
> *rest your hope fully upon the grace that is to be brought*
> *to you at the revelation of Jesus Christ.* (1 Peter 1:13)

Grace should be the basis of our hope at the return of Jesus. If it were not for grace and its work in our lives, we could never hope to endure the appearing of such a holy God. Our hope is in grace and not in our hard work, our sincere efforts, or our devotion to doctrine. If not for grace and its unmerited character, we wouldn't welcome Jesus; we'd shrink back from His presence. Our sin and shame would be laid bare in all their blackness next to His absolute purity, and we'd be like those described in the book of Revelation who beg for the rocks to cover them in a vain attempt to hide from His holiness (Rev. 6:16).

Getting ready for Jesus' second coming is a work God does in us, and we can then rest in His grace and work together with it. The key is abiding in the God of all grace and trusting in His promise to prepare us for that day. Left to our own efforts, we'd never be ready.

Peter's encouragement to set our hope upon this grace to come is presented in the context of a challenge to right living. The promise of future grace is given in the midst of a call to holiness:

> *As obedient children, not conforming yourselves to the*
> *former lusts, as in your ignorance; but as He who called*
> *you is holy, you also be holy in all your conduct, because*
> *it is written, "Be holy, for I am holy."* (1 Peter 1:14-
> 16)

Some people may think that a call to holiness doesn't belong in the same passage that speaks of the great grace that will be brought to us at the appearing of our Lord. But Peter understood that as we fully realize our destiny, we become more passionate in our pursuit of it. As we understand that by grace God is committed to seeing us through to the end, we gain courage and strength to pursue the race. It's wrong to think that grace excuses us from pursuing holiness. Rather, true grace, properly received and understood, frees us to pursue holy living more diligently and effectively.

The work grace does in preparing us to meet Jesus at His appearing is a remarkable thing. However, the plan of grace extends beyond the day of His return, far into eternity future. God's eternal purpose in the ages to come is to show the exceeding riches of His grace toward us. As the apostle Paul wrote:

> *That in the ages to come He might show the exceeding riches of His grace in His kindness toward us in Christ Jesus.* (Eph. 2:7)

One of God's great purposes in our salvation is to show forth His grace in all its glory. Within the plan of grace, God gets all the credit and all the glory for the salvation of man. If man could be saved by the system of Law, then he could rightly take some of the credit for salvation, but under the plan of grace, only the merits of Jesus are recognized. We can't even take the credit for the faith that enabled us to receive the grace of God, because even that is the gift of God (Eph. 2:8).

Understanding this, we can see how offensive it must be to God when some make salvation a matter of works and not grace. If salvation were possible under a system of works, then man could rightfully take some of the credit and glory. Such a strategy frustrates God's plan to reveal His glory by making salvation available only as a free gift to be received in Jesus Christ.

We can be confident that in the wonders of the coming age, God will find new and greater ways to give glory to His grace. God's plan of grace will keep amazing us in eternity future.

Grace isn't a temporary method of God's dealing with man; it's His eternal plan and purpose. We don't have to worry whether He'll change the rules on us because His plan for us begins, continues, and finishes in grace.

An Eternal Plan

It isn't hard to figure out what God wants from this plan of grace. He simply desires that many would receive His grace, giving greater glory to the God who gave it. When more people honor God's plan of grace, He receives more glory from those created in His image. God wants all people to praise and worship Him, the God of all grace, and He wants grace to be a place of rest, sure footing, and victory for the believer.

Appendix

A FEW WORDS ABOUT GRACE by William Newell[77]

I. *The Nature of Grace*

1. Grace is God acting freely, according to His own nature as Love; with no promises or obligations to fulfill; and acting of course, righteously—in view of the cross.

2. Grace, therefore, is *uncaused* in the recipient: its cause lies wholly in the *GIVER,* in *GOD.*

3. Grace, also is *sovereign.* Not having debts to pay, or fulfilled conditions on man's part to wait for, it can act toward whom, and how, it pleases. It can, and does, often, place the worst deservers in the highest favors.

4. Grace cannot act where there is either *desert* or *ability:* Grace does not *help*—it is *absolute,* it *does all.*

5. There being *no cause* in the creature why Grace should be shown, the creature must be brought off from *trying to give cause* to God for His Grace.

6. The discovery by the creature that he is truly the object of Divine grace, works the *utmost humility:* for the receiver of grace is brought to know his own absolute unworthiness, and his complete

inability to attain worthiness: yet he finds himself blessed—*on another principal, outside of himself!*

7. Therefore, *flesh has no place* in the plan of Grace. This is *the great reason why Grace is hated* by the proud natural mind of man. But for this very reason, the true believer rejoices! For he knows that "in him, that is, in his flesh, is no good thing"; and yet he finds God glad to bless him, just as he is!

II. *The Place of Man under Grace*

1. He has been accepted *in Christ,* who *is* his standing!

2. He is not "on probation."

3. As to his life past, *it does not exist* before God: he *died* at the Cross, and *Christ is his life.*

4. Grace, once bestowed, is *not withdrawn*: for God knew all the human exigencies beforehand: His action was independent of them, not dependent upon them.

5. The failure of devotion does not cause the withdrawal of bestowed grace (as it would under law). For example: the man in 1 Cor. 5:1-5; and also those in 11:30-32, who did not "judge" themselves, and so were "judged by the Lord,—that they might *not* be condemned with the world"!

III. *The Proper Attitude of Man under Grace*

1. To *believe*, and consent to be *loved while unworthy,* is the great secret.

2. To refuse to make "resolutions" and "vows"; for that is to trust in the flesh.

3. To expect to be blessed, though realizing more and more lack of worth.

4. To testify of God's goodness, at all times.

5. To be certain of God's future favor; yet to be ever more tender in conscience toward Him.

6. To rely on God's chastening hand as a mark of His kindness.

7. A man under grace, if like Paul, has no burdens regarding himself; but many about others.

IV. *Things Which Gracious Souls Discover*

1. To "hope to be better" is to fail to see yourself *in Christ only.*

2. To be *disappointed* with yourself, is to have *believed* in yourself.

3. To be *discouraged* is *unbelief,*—as to God's purpose and plan of blessing for you.

4. To be *proud,* is to be *blind!* For we have no standing before God, in *ourselves.*

5. The lack of Divine blessing, therefore, comes from *unbelief,* and not from *failure of devotion.*

6. Real *devotion* to God arises, not from *man's will* to show it; but from the discovery that blessing *has been received* from God while we were yet *unworthy and undevoted.*

7. To preach devotion first, and blessing second, is to reverse God's order, and preach *law, not grace.* The Law made man's blessing depend on devotion; Grace *confers undeserved, unconditional blessing*: our devotion may follow, but does not always do so,—in proper measure.

Chapter Notes

Chapter 1

1. Wendell W. Watters, "Christianity and Mental Health," *The Humanist* (November/December 1987), pages 5-11.

2. Ibid, page 5.

3. Ibid, page 8.

4. Ibid, page 10.

5. Ibid, pages 7, 10, and 7.

6. Ibid, page 8.

7. Alexander Maclaren, *Expositions of Holy Scripture* volume 15 (Grand Rapids: Baker Book House, 1984), pages 141-142.

8. Charles Spurgeon, "Paul's Parenthesis," *The Metropolitan Tabernacle Pulpit, Volume 54* (Pasadena, Texas: Pilgrim Publications, 1978) page 140.

9. James Moffatt, *Grace in the New Testament* (London: Hodder and Stoughton, 1931), page 392.

Chapter 2

10. Steven Turner, *Amazing Grace: The Story of America's Most Beloved Song* (New York: Harper Collins, 2003), page 196.

11. Ibid, page 186.

12. Ibid, page xxvii.

13. A. Morgan Derham, "Newton, John" *The New International Dictionary of the Christian Church* (Grand Rapids: Zondervan, 1974).

14. Turner, page 108.

15. This line from Augustine is often attributed to him, but without citation.

16. Associated Press as reported in *The New York Times*, "Reagan Tells of Gaffe with Mrs. Mitterrand" April 7, 1984.

17. Charles Caldwell Ryrie, *The Grace of God* (Chicago: Moody Press, 1963), page 20.

18. Moffatt, page 21.

19. Ibid, page 28.

20. Ibid, page 25.

21. Aristotle cited by Moffatt, page 25.

22. Kenneth S. Wuest, *Philippians: in the Greek New Testament*, (Grand Rapids, Michigan WM. B. Eerdmans Publishing Co., 1951), page 29.

23. G. Campbell Morgan *The Corinthian Letters of Paul* (Old Tappan, New Jersey: Fleming H. Revell, 1946), page 251.

24. Wuest, page 29.

25. Moffatt, page xv.

26. Ryrie, page 9.

27. Moffatt, page 9.

28. Ryrie, page 28.

29. Oscar Hardman, *The Christian Doctrine of Grace*, (New York: Macmillan, 1947), page 11.

30. Alan Redpath, *Blessings out of Buffetings*, (Grand Rapids, Michigan: Fleming H. Revell, 1993) page 154.

Chapter 3

31. Clifton Fadiman, *The Little, Brown Book of Anecdotes* (Boston: Little, Brown, and Company, 1985) page 357.

32. "United States v. Wilson," https://en.wikipedia.org/wiki/United_States_v._Wilson

33. Moffatt, page 7.

34. Ibid, page 132.

Chapter 4

35. Fadiman, page 188.

36. Thomas Torrance, *The Doctrine of Grace in the Apostolic Fathers* (Grand Rapids: Eerdmans, 1948), page 39.

37. Moffatt, page 132.

38. Leon Morris, *The Epistle to the Romans* (Grand Rapids: Eerdmans, 1988), page 219.

39. Kenneth S. Wuest, *Romans in The Greek New Testament* (Grand Rapids: Eerdmans, 1955), page 78.

40. Charles Spurgeon, "Growth in Grace," *The Metropolitan Tabernacle Pulpit, Volume 46* (Pasadena, Texas: Pilgrim Publications, 1977) page 530.

41. Moffatt, page 30.

42. Ibid, page 31.

43. Lewis Chafer, *Grace, The Glorious Theme* (Grand Rapids: Zondervan, 1922), page 157.

Chapter 5

44. Fadiman, pages 588-589.

45. Ibid, page 248.

46. This nursery rhyme or song has several variations. Examples can be found at https://100.best-poems.net/nobody-likes-me-guess-i039ll-go-eat-worms.html and http://www.mamalisa.com/?t=es&p=2387

47. Fadiman, page 169.

48. https://en.wikipedia.org/wiki/The_Last_Supper_(Leonardo_da_Vinci)

49. D. Martin Lloyd-Jones, *God's Ultimate Purpose* (Grand Rapids: Baker, 1979), page 136.

50. From a story told by Booker T. Washington (1903 recording) http://historymatters.gmu.edu/d/88/

51. Martin Luther, *A Commentary on St. Paul's Epistle to the Galatians* (Grand Rapids: Zondervan, 1937) page 158.

Chapter 6

52. See Kenneth Wuest, *The New Testament – An Expanded Translation* (Grand Rapids: Eerdmans, 1961) page 360 and Morris, page 242.

53. Augustine, found in *A Library of the Fathers of the Holy Catholic Church*, (Oxford: John Henry Parker, 1847) page 248.

54. Thomas Brooks, "A Cabinet of Jewels," *The Works of Thomas Brooks, Volume III* (Edinburgh: James Nichol, 1866) page 318.

55. Dietrich Bonhoeffer, *The Cost of Discipleship* (New York: Macmillan, 1979) pages 45-46.

56. Charles Spurgeon, "The World on Fire," *The Metropolitan Tabernacle Pulpit, Volume 19* (Pasadena, Texas: Pilgrim Publications, 1981) page 441.

Chapter 7

57. Kenneth S. Wuest, *Romans in The Greek New Testament* (Grand Rapids: Eerdmans, 1955), pages 109-111.

58. From International Movie Database: http://www.imdb.com/title/ tt0054331/trivia?tab=qt&ref_=tt_trv_qu

59. Thomas B. Costain, *The Three Edwards* (Garden City, New York: Doubleday & Company, 1958), pages 179-180.

60. Dwight Lyman Moody, *Moody's Anecdotes* (Chicago: Rhodes & McClure Publishing Co., 1896), pages 144-145.

61. Redpath, page 236.

62. Edward Cardwell, *Syodalia – A Collection of Articles of Religions, Canons, and Proceedings of Convocations, Volume 1* (Oxford: The University Press, 1842), page 21.

63. Charles Spurgeon, "The Safeguards of Forgiveness," *The Metropolitan Tabernacle Pulpit, Volume 52* (Pasadena, Texas: Pilgrim Publications, 1978) page 163.

64. John Bunyan, *The Pilgrim's Progress* (Grand Rapids: Baker, 1978), pages 389-390.

Chapter 8

65. Fadiman, page 383.

Chapter 9

66. Sergei Kourdakov, *Sergei* (London: Oliphants, 1973).

Chapter 10

67. See Kenneth Scott Latourette, *A History of Christianity Volume 1* (Peabody, Massachusetts, Prince Press, 1997) pages 137-138.

68. Charles Spurgeon, "Lessons on Divine Grace," *The Metropolitan Tabernacle Pulpit, Volume 49* (Pasadena, Texas: Pilgrim Publications, 1977) page 256.

Chapter 11

69. Maclaren, page 335.

Chapter 12

70. C.S. Lewis, *Mere Christianity*, (New York: Macmillan, 1943), page 109.

71. Ibid, pages 111-112.

72. Oscar Hardman, *The Christian Doctrine of Grace* (New York: The Macmillan Company, 1947) page 11.

73. Torrance, page 141.

74. Ibid.

75. Charles Spurgeon, "The Danger of Unconfessed Sin," *The Metropolitan Tabernacle Pulpit, Volume 23* (Pasadena, Texas: Pilgrim Publications, 1979) page 426.

Chapter 13

76. Charles Spurgeon, "Growth in Grace," *The Metropolitan Tabernacle Pulpit, Volume 46* (Pasadena, Texas: Pilgrim Publications, 1977) page 530.

Appendix

77. William R. Newell, *Romans Verse by Verse* (Chicago: Moody Press, 1979), pages 245-249.

Author's Remarks

This book was started sometime in the mid 1980s, coming out of a profound work of God's grace in my life. I earnestly hope that the message of grace that touched me so deeply will also touch some others.

Over the years that this book was in my mind and jumbled up on a computer, God has shown His grace to me so wonderfully in Jesus Christ and through His Word; beyond that, also in many ways and through many people. Of those people, none has shown me more grace and goodness than my wonderful and precious wife Inga-Lill. There is really no one else to whom I could possibly dedicate this book to. Thank you, Inga-Lill.

Some others deserve some special acknowledgement:

- Debbie Pollaccia for her invaluable proofreading work.

- Lance Ralston for not letting me forget this manuscript.

- My many friends and colleagues in serving God over the years.

- This revised edition owes a special debt of gratitude to Nancy Aguilar, whose editorial and review work made this book *much* better.

- The cover of this revised edition was designed by Brian Procedo, whose work I heartily recommend. Contact him at brian@brianprocedo.com

With each year that passes, faithful friends and supporters become all the more precious. Through you all, God has been better to me than I have ever deserved.

David Guzik is a pastor, author, and Bible commentator. David and his wife Inga-Lill live in Santa Barbara, California. David's online commentary on the entire Bible is a helpful resources for many pastors, teachers, and everyday Christians and can be found at

enduringword.com

CPSIA information can be obtained
at www.ICGtesting.com
Printed in the USA
BVHW071923040121
596832BV00004B/445